Unlocking the Reader
in Every Child

Pleas

About the author

Susan Elkin is an education journalist, former secondary school English teacher and author of 25 books. She has worked for many years to promote and develop pupils' reading at all levels.

Also in this series

Why 'Literacy' Sucks
  - and what we're going to have to do about it
                              Stephen Rickard
                              978-184167-975-4

Unlocking the Reader
in Every Child

THE book of practical ideas for teaching reading

Susan Elkin

Ransom

Unlocking the Reader in Every Child

by Susan Elkin

Published by Ransom Publishing Ltd.

Radley House, 8 St. Cross Road, Winchester, Hants. SO23 9HX, UK

www.ransom.co.uk

ISBN   978 184167 970 9

First published in 2010

Contents

A note

In this book I sometimes talk about letters we read on the page (such as the letters oa in 'boat', as well as letter sounds that we make (such as the sh sound in 'shop').

To avoid confusion, I have adopted the following convention throughout the book:

Letters and combinations of letters (i.e. *as written*) are shown in single apostrophes – 'o', 'oa', 'ing', and so on.

Sounds (*as heard*) are shown in italics, with a single '/' before and after the sound – */oa/*, */sh/*, */th/*, etc.

I hope this will reduce confusion.

 Introduction

> *Dit is een book over het leren lezen.*
>
> *Este é urn livro sobre ensino leitura.*

The first sentence is Dutch. The second is Portuguese. If you happen to know either language you will have read *'This is a book about reading.'*

Otherwise you simply saw unfamiliar organisations of letters into words which you couldn't pronounce, and which had little or no meaning for you, although there is one word – 'book' – in the first sentence which is the same in Dutch as in English.

Look very closely at this little rhyme.

> *Zkk zkk zfkju pwiid*
> *Wkai msn kem lssf?*
> *Mip pvc, mip pvc*
> *Bwcii zkhp xnff.*

You just might recognise the patterns of *Baa Baa Black Sheep* in code, although I wouldn't blame you if you didn't, because it looks like gibberish. (The encoded alphabet runs K Z J Y I X H W V G U F T E S D R C P B N A L O M Q.)

These are exactly the kind of puzzles we set young children every day when we present them with printed text and expect them to read it.

Reading is a highly sophisticated skill.

First you have to make some sense out of the squiggles on the page. You have to recognise each letter and understand how they are put together to make words. What do these words actually say? How do they sound when spoken aloud?

Second, you have to understand what these words mean in this order and in this context. What is being said?

It's no wonder that so many children find it so difficult.

 Psychologists still do not fully understand how children do learn to read. A few children seem to grasp it effortlessly and with very little help, whilst many succeed only after considerable effort.

Others, especially boys, struggle and quickly fall behind.

Learning to read is a chore – and it's not achieved quickly – but reading itself is (for most of us) a pleasure.

So how do we teach children to read without putting them off books and reading in general? It's an age-old problem for which this book tries to suggest some solutions.

Is this book for you?

Many academic books have been written about teaching reading, but this is not one of them.

My aim in this book is twofold:

1 to provide a basic, quick-to-read guide to teaching reading. This includes something about how written English is put together, and the difficulties children face in learning to read; and

2 to suggest some practical 'try this' ideas to help overcome obstacles and perhaps give some fresh perspectives.

So I will be moving (effortlessly!) from quick overviews to very 'hands on' things to try out. For this reason, most of the chapters in this book are divided into two parts: first, a quick outline of some of the key issues; followed by a section containing practical teaching ideas.

I hope this book will help teachers, special needs co-ordinators, and anyone else working in schools (such as learning support assistants, teaching assistants and volunteers who help with reading and encouraging reading).

But this is not just a book for teachers.

Are you a parent or guardian trying to encourage your children to read? Or are you simply concerned that your children may not be progressing at the rate that they should – and in the right way?

If you are wondering how much books still matter in this digital age, consider this:

In 2003 a study in 37 countries by the Programme for International Student Assessment (PISA) found that the most important factor for academic success was the amount of time pupils spent reading – books, magazines, newspapers and websites. But it's time spent reading books which makes the biggest difference – according to this and several other studies.

If so, you are probably needing information about how literacy teaching works – in which case this book is for you, too.

> **We all want to do the best we can to help our children, and developing effective literacy is probably the most important skill they will ever learn.**

Remember though that no two children are the same and every teacher is different. One size most definitely does not fit all. That is why it's useful to have plenty of strategies for getting reluctant readers excited by reading. What works for one child in one classroom with a particular teacher or adult won't necessarily work in a different situation.

So we have to find ways of meeting individual needs. And parents, at home, of course are better placed than anyone to do just that. So don't be afraid to get involved if you want to help your own children.

 We also have to develop ways of encouraging and developing reading once a child has cracked the code.

That is the moment to turn children into *real readers* as opposed to laborious decipherers who *can* read, but not fluently or fast enough for it yet to have become an established life-long habit.

Part One of this book deals with the mechanics of how children learn – and can be taught – to decode the squiggles they see on the page. Part Two is about helping children grow into effortless readers of everything they need, or want, to read. It also suggests ways of developing specific aspects of literacy, such as poetry and non-fiction.

Let's start with how written English works.

Part One

The Mechanics of Learning to Read

1 Welcome to English

1 Welcome to English

 The Issues

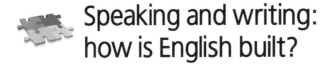 ## Speaking and writing: how is English built?

There are 26 letters in the English alphabet. But when we speak English, we make up words from about 44 different, distinct speech sounds (the exact number varies, depending upon regional accents). These distinct speech sounds are known as **phonemes**. (You can think of a phoneme as the smallest meaningful sound in our language.)

So clearly there's a problem. When it comes to writing down what we say, how do we represent all of the 44 phonemes when we have only 26 letters to work with?

The answer, of course, is to use combinations of letters to represent individual phonemes.

 So, for example, the letter 'o' denotes the /o/ sound in *pot*, but putting two 'o's together gives us the /oo/ sound in *look*.

By combining letters in this way we are able to write words depicting all of the 44 phonemes, or speech sounds, that we make.

 So the /sh/ sound in *shop* is a single phoneme. So is the /ch/ sound in *such*, the /th/ sound in *than* and the /oa/ in *coat*. Each of these sounds needs two letters to represent it in writing.

Just as each individual speech sound is called a phoneme, its written equivalent on the page is called a **grapheme**. So the 'o' in *pot* is a grapheme, as is the 'oo' in *look*. (The 'p', 't', 'l' and 'k' in these words are of course graphemes, too.)

When a grapheme consists of two letters (as 'oa' in *coat*) it is called a **digraph**.

But remember – a grapheme is the written representation of a phoneme. So the 'oa' in *coat* is a two-letter grapheme, or digraph, because the 'oa' is the written representation of a single phoneme – the /oa/ sound. But the two letters 't' and 'r' in *trap* are not a digraph – because they represent two separate phonemes (/t/ and /r/) which are simply sounded quickly one after the other (or *blended*) in the word *trap*.

Parents: don't be surprised if your children know the terms *grapheme*, *phoneme* and *digraph*. They are encouraged at school to be familiar with these names, as well as what they mean.

Every word we speak consists of a combination of these 44 phonemes, and every word we write uses a combination of graphemes to represent these speech sounds.

Twenty four of the English language's 44 phonemes are consonant sounds, such as /c/, /b/, /d/, /f/ and /s/.

The remaining 20 phonemes are vowel sounds, such as the sounds (ignore the spelling and hear the sound): /ee/, /ay/, /oo/ and so on.

Phonics

This all takes us into the world of phonics. Phonics is a system of teaching reading by training the reader to recognise graphemes in written text and to associate them with their corresponding phonemes, or sounds in speech, exactly in the way described above.

Teaching reading using a phonics approach in this way capitalises on the fact that English is an alphabetic language. You can't use phonics to teach people to read Chinese, for example, since it is not based on an alphabet.

> The word 'phonics' comes from the Greek word for sound or voice (think of 'tele**phone**' 'eu**phon**ium' and 'sym**phon**y').

The advantage of a phonics-based approach in teaching is that once you have learned the basics, you should be able successfully to read words that you have never encountered before.

Phonics seems complicated because it often uses a lot of off-putting technical terms, but the principles are actually very simple.

English is not regular

So based on what we have talked about so far, a phonics-based approach to learning to read should be easy. With 26 letters in the alphabet, and another 18 digraphs (that is, two-letter combinations) making up the rest of the 44 sounds in English, we should be able to write all that we hear – and it's all plain sailing …

Well … no. Unfortunately it's just not that simple.

The English language has evolved over 2,000 years, with an unusually wide range of outside influences. The Celts were already speaking an ancient language when the Romans arrived to occupy Britain for over 400 years. The Romans had a big impact upon the language, and a few very old words from

Reading with children from an early age undoubtedly helps develop their literacy skills.

original Latin – *vinegar* for instance – are still in use in their original form in modern English.

Subsequent invasions by Vikings, Angles, Jutes, Saxons and others during the so-called 'Dark Ages' brought us their languages, as well as the more famous rape and pillage. From this melting pot developed Old English, with words such as *sheep, ox, earth* and *plough*.

In 1066 the Normans turned up with their Latin-based Norman French, which eventually merged with the language known as Old English. About half the words we use today are derived from Latin via Norman French.

Then, beginning in the sixteenth century, the British travelled all over the world 'discovering' new (to them) lands and establishing colonies. Wherever they went they absorbed new words into the language. There are plenty of examples.

Bungalow is a Hindi word, *kangaroo* is from Australia. *Safari* comes from Swahili and *potato* from Spanish (because Spain ruled in South America where Sir Walter Raleigh found the humble spud and brought it to Britain in the sixteenth century.)

The result is that this glorious mish-mash of a language that is English has picked up some odd grammatical structures and some even more quirky spellings. This makes written English unusually irregular.

 One mouse, two *mice*: so why do we have two *houses*, rather than two *hice*? And why is the plural of sheep ... *sheep*?

For example, many letter sounds, or phonemes, can be represented in writing by several different graphemes.

 Take the /*ay*/ phoneme – the vowel sound in the word *pay*. It can also be written as:

'eigh'	(*neigh, eight*)
'a_e'	(*rate, late*)
'ai'	(*paid, raid*)
'ei'	(*rein*)
'a'	(*acorn*) or
'ey'	(*they*).

And the /*sh*/ phoneme can be written

'sh'	(*hush*)
'c'	(*special*)
't'	(*station*)
's'	(*sure*)
'ss'	(*passion*) or
'ch'	(*chef* or *Michelle*).

These are not a few rare examples, either. It is very common, and some of the most common words used in English (so-called 'high frequency words') suffer from this 'inconsistency'.

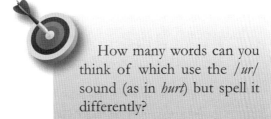

How many words can you think of which use the /ur/ sound (as in *hurt*) but spell it differently?

It cuts both ways, too. Just as there are a number of ways of *writing* a particular phoneme, so there are a number of ways of sounding out, or *speaking*, a particular grapheme.

 When you read, for example, the grapheme 'ea' it relates to different phonemes in *bread, bead, bear* and *fear.*

And we can find words to rhyme with each of those which are spelled differently (*said* rhymes with *bread, feed* with *bead, care* with *bear* and *beer* with *fear*).

So the 'ea' spelling can represent a number of different phonemes, or sounds. And many of those phonemes have more than one grapheme. If you find that confusing – it's because it is.

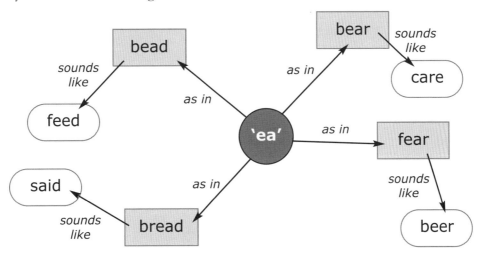

The written grapheme 'ea' has four different sounds, or phonemes. Each of those sounds can be represented by at least two graphemes.

You can probably begin to see why English is a difficult language to read, write and spell.

 # How do we learn to read?

We don't *really* know how children (or anybody else) learns to read. We have ideas, we have some theories, and we know what tends to help and what doesn't. But, beyond that, it all gets a bit foggy.

For as long as I can remember, experts have argued (sometimes bitterly) about which is the best approach to teaching reading. The argument still goes on today.

The discussion of phonemes and graphemes at the beginning of this chapter is something a teacher of fifty years ago might not recognise – or regard as important. A phonics-based approach to teaching reading is only one of a number of methods – and fifty years ago, phonics was out of favour.

 Don't despair. The vast majority of children learn to read very well and master reading astonishingly quickly, despite the language's apparent complications.

But before we focus on how to teach children to read, let's look at how children themselves learn.

First of all, children don't all learn in the same way. Every child is different and what works for one may not work for another – a point I shall keep coming back to.

None of us reads using just one method of understanding text anyway. When you, as an adult, glance in the rear-view mirror in your car and see the word **Police** on the vehicle behind, you don't break it down (or 'decode' it) phonetically. You recognise the whole word shape and read it one go – a technique known as 'sight-reading' or 'whole-word recognition' – learning to read a word simply by recognising its shape.

I once taught a most unfortunate child whose parents had saddled her with the name Gentilia. Almost every adult who saw her name on a register or list initially misread it.

Think about it! (And be careful when you think about naming your children.)

On the other hand, if you come across a long or complex word which is new to you, then you probably do break it down in order to pronounce it. I met the word *obnubilate* the other day for the first time. It means to cloud or obscure and I had to look at it quite closely to read it.

Sight-reading is not a fashionable approach to the teaching of reading these days, but we do all do it. Children learn to recognise words by sight, whether they have been taught to do it or not.

 Give almost any young boy a book on dinosaurs and he'll find the words *Tyrannosaurus Rex* – even though phonetically they are well beyond his reading ability. Somehow he just knows.

Another example comes from football (or any sport for that matter). Children will follow their favourite team and often look up their team's standing in the league tables. They always seem to be able to find their team – even if the team has a difficult name like *Leicester City* or *Middlesbrough*.

And there are, of course, many very ordinary words that children have to learn early on which can only be sight-read, because they are not phonetically decodable. These include words such as *the, through, one, should, two, ought, are, where* – and dozens more. Many of them are the everyday connecting words we use to turn words into sentences.

Take another example. If you present, say, a six year-old with some text full of unfamiliar words, they will quickly give up – but they will, almost certainly, take a few words in their stride. Isn't it the same for adults? I quite often see a new word in my reading, but it doesn't put me off reading the rest of the page. I simply ignore it and sail on (perhaps looking it up later when I have a minute, but maybe not). As long as it doesn't happen too often, it spoils neither my understanding nor my pleasure. That is healthy reading!

> It's hard to avoid the conclusion that, when we read, we use a variety of techniques to understand the words that we see. Breaking words down, decoding and sight-reading all seem to play a part.

 # Ways of teaching reading

Those of us who have been teaching for a while have seen a number of different teaching methods come and go over the years. Each still has something to offer today, so it's useful quickly to run through these different approaches.

In fact, all the various methods can be divided into two broad categories: 'top-down' and 'bottom-up'.

 ### Top-down 1: Whole-language

In the 1960s, 70s and 80s it was common to teach reading using a **whole-language** approach. The idea behind this approach is that reading should be meaning-based, so that when children meet an unfamiliar word, they look at it as a whole unit and infer its meaning from the context (i.e. the rest of the words in the sentence, what the text or story is about and any associated pictures).

> This method places little value on looking at how the words themselves are constructed, or put together.

At the same time, it was also popular to teach reading using flashcards. This was a formal reinforcement of the whole-language approach. It meant having words written on cards, showing them to the children and training them to recognise the shapes of the words. This is whole-word recognition.

Flashcards.

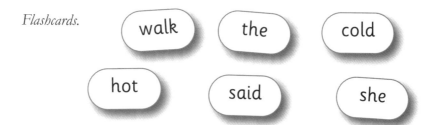

 Whole-word recognition worked well for some words – especially long, interesting words with a distinctive shape, like *elephant* or *magician*.

It was also a good way of learning to recognise the child's own name in cases such as *Katherine, Arthur, Michael* or *Penelope*, where the names are not phonetically spelled; or the un-phonetic town in which the child might live – such as *Torquay, Wellingborough, Llangollen* or *St Andrews.*

Critics of the flashcard method of teaching reading said, with justification, that used on its own it was very limiting and that as a result many children failed to learn to read.

A child would be able to read only the words that they had seen and learned before. There was no taught strategy for deducing what words said or meant.

So there was no sense of learning one word, such as *cart*, and using it as a pivot to generate knowledge of lots of other words such as *dart, artist, starter, part* and so on. As a result guesswork came to play a big part.

 Reading schemes such as *Ladybird, Janet and John* and the *Beacon Readers* all worked mainly on whole-word recognition. This time, as the words were in books, they were being read in some sort of context rather than being read in isolation (as with flashcards).

Top-down 2: Real books

Then there was a movement against reading schemes. Some teachers, and others, argued for the teaching of reading using *real books*. They believed that if you gave a child an abundant supply of good quality books at the right level and read these books to, and with, the child on a daily basis, then they would simply pick up reading by natural absorption.

Some children indeed did, but others did not.

Opponents of real books (as a method of teaching reading) countered that, at best, this was teaching a child to read by guesswork and looking at pictures. Far too many children, they said, simply failed to learn to read at all, except very late and without fluency.

So this approach fell out of favour.

 ### Top down 3: Analytic phonics

Analytic phonics is a phonics-based approach, but the child is taught to look at individual words and break them down – or *analyse* them – in order to read them.

> Because it is a phonics-based approach, analytic phonics requires children to have some phonological awareness (i.e. the ability to hear and discriminate sounds in spoken words).

Analytic phonics avoids many of the limitations of the whole-language, flashcard and real book approaches described above. But it is still a 'top-down' approach.

Analytic phonics involves analysing whole words to identify patterns, then splitting the words into smaller parts to help with decoding.

Onset and **rime** play a big part in analytic phonics. The onset of a word is the beginning part, and rime the ending part.

 Analytic phonics works particularly well for words that young children cannot work out sound-by-sound – words like *fight, through* and *take.*

Children are taught to hear (and discriminate) both the onset and the rime in words. For example, take the word *clock*. Children learning to listen soon hear that the /*cl*/ sound is also the onset of *clay, clever, cliff* and *clutter*.

 Once children can hear the onset /*d*/ in *dog*, they can associate it with the same sound at the onset of *doll, digger, dentist, dalek, duck* and so on.

This is why rhymes which use alliteration (words starting with the same letters or sounds) such as *Peter Piper picked a peck of pickled pepper* are useful.

The rime is usually taught to children as beginning with a vowel (*-ing, -ast, -alk*). This makes it easier to identify the word ending.

Identifying the rimes of words is an efficient way to help children develop a large sight vocabulary for both reading and spelling. It is also effective in helping children become familiar with the common sight words, however irregular they are.

Bottom-up: synthetic phonics

The main 'bottom-up' approach to teaching reading is synthetic phonics. It involves children putting together, or *synthesising*, words from component letters and clusters of letters.

Synthetic phonics is usually taught systematically. In other words, rather than tackling words as children meet them in their reading, synthetic phonics starts by gradually introducing the *components* of words – the phonemes and graphemes – and carefully controlling the vocabulary (i.e. the words) that the children are exposed to.

Most schools follow a synthetic phonics *programme* – a structured approach to teaching that carefully controls how and when new phonemes and graphemes are introduced.

All the synthetic phonics programmes are basically similar. They introduce the children to graphemes, phonemes and grapheme-phoneme correspondences on a carefully managed and staged basis – often at the rate of one new grapheme a day.

There are now about 20 synthetic phonics programmes on the market, which schools (and parents) can use.

These include *Jolly Phonics*, which was a bit of a trailblazer in the early 1990s and influenced most of the others. Another scheme, *Letters and Sounds*, was produced by the UK Government and is available free of charge.

Children learn to relate specific graphemes (e.g. the letter 'o') with specific phonemes (e.g. the sound /o/ as in *pot*). These correspondences are referred to as **grapheme-phoneme correspondences**, or GPCs).

Most programmes start with a few simple letters (strictly speaking, they are graphemes) such as 's', 'a', 't', 'p', 'i' and 'n'. Children learn these GPCs and start building simple words (*cat*, *sat*, *pit*, etc.). These words are known

Working with letters is an essential part of phonics-based teaching.

as CVC (consonant-vowel-consonant) words because that's how they're built up.

Children quickly progress to blending these phonemes and it's wonderful to see the penny drop when a child first realises that you can put /m/ /a/ and /t/ together to make *mat*.

From there it is a very short step to their seeing *mat* written and realising that they can read it.

Even if they don't recognise it, they can work out what it says – heady stuff, when you are four or five!

Gradually more (and more complex) letter sounds are introduced and more complex words are built. For example, some digraph sounds are introduced (e.g. /ai/ as in *rain*, /ch/ as in *chip*) as well as CCVC words (*snip*, *trap*) and CCVCC words (*think*, *shark*), etc.

 The key advantage of the synthetic phonics approach is that it is systematic. Children should, in theory at least, be able to read, or 'decode', any word which is made out of graphemes and phonemes that they have met so far – even if they have never seen the word before. So, if they have met 's', 'ai', 't', and 'r', they will be able to read the word *straits*, even if they have never seen it before.

Generally speaking, in a synthetic phonics approach, the more irregular forms of English (discussed earlier) are introduced towards the end.

There is no doubt that synthetic phonics is a powerful and effective way of teaching many – if not most – children the basics of literacy. It is also right that we have seen the pendulum swing away from whole-word approaches, to now placing more emphasis on a bottom-up approach.

However, synthetic phonics is not a universal panacea. It does have its shortcomings.

It does, for example, place the emphasis clearly on the decoding of text – arguably at the expense of comprehension and of simple, enjoyable reading.

Synthetic phonics works well for words that are phonetically regular, such as *start, fat* or *market.*

It is less helpful with words with silent letters and other phonetic irregularities, such as *gnome, Charlotte* or *Leicester.*

Nevertheless, it does work very well with many – if not most – children, although it may not be the best approach for all.

In 2006 in the United Kingdom, Sir Jim Rose completed a report on how reading should be taught in UK schools. Based on evidence from a case study in Scotland, the report concluded that synthetic phonics-based teaching leads to better reading and spelling than other approaches.

With effect from autumn 2007, as a direct result of the Rose report, the teaching of reading in schools using a synthetic phonics programme became compulsory in all English schools, with the exception of private and independent schools.

It seems therefore that the best approach to teaching the basics of literacy is one based on synthetic phonics, but recognising that children themselves use other approaches – in combination – when decoding texts.

1 Welcome to English

Practical Teaching Ideas

Building phonological awareness

A child cannot begin to learn to read using phonics until they have what experts call 'phonological awareness'. That means, as we have seen, an ability to hear the different sounds in a word – such as hearing and knowing that *lamb, lion, Lisa* and *London* all start with the same sound; or that *box, socks,* and *forks* all end with the same sound (even though spelled differently).

> Children have to learn to *listen* and to *hear* (not quite the same thing) before they can learn to read.

Indeed, the first stage of most synthetic phonics programmes involves teaching children to listen to and discriminate different sounds – without any reference to reading or even to the letters of the alphabet.

There is a lot that parents can do to develop these skills, long before the child goes to school. Here are a few activities to get you started. They are great fun both at home and at school.

Alliterative tongue-twisters

✎ A few alliterative tongue-twisters are always fun to play with – and they build phonological awareness. Here are a few suggestions:

> *Ben Brown bought a buttered biscuit.*
>
> *Jasmine, Jack and Jade jiggle their jigsaws.*
>
> *Felix, Freddy and Fergus feed the fish.*
>
> *Harriet and Henry hate hats.*

These are not difficult to make up.

✎ You can extend this activity by asking the children to make up some tongue-twisters of their own. This should be done orally/aurally, without writing anything down: it's the *sound* that matters, not the spelling. For example:

> *Cyril sat sipping cider.*
>
> *Funny Phyllis phoned Felicity.*

✎ If you are working with a group of children, you could extend this activity by asking one child to start with the first word, then asking each child in turn to add a word (alliterative, of course), repeating the whole sentence (so far) as they go.

This usually causes great hilarity as the sentence gets sillier and sillier as more words are added:

> *Silly ... Sid ... said ... sad ... stones ... still ... seem ... strangely ... strong ...*

You can play this game with older reluctant readers, too: you just need to invent some snappy, up-to-date tongue-twisters which are not 'babyish':

> *Max meant to mend his mum's mobile.*
>
> *Freddie Ferguson is a frightening football freak.*

> When you are trying to develop phonological awareness through rhyme, concentrate on sound. Ignore pairs of words like *fork/work*, *rough/cough*, *comb/tomb*, *come/home*.
>
> These are known as 'eye rhymes'. Written down they may look like rhymes, but in modern English, at least, they do not sound as rhymes, apart from the final letter.

Play with rhyming sounds

 Words which end with the same sound – various forms of rhyme – help children to listen to the sounds of language too. It's why nursery rhymes and poems are crucial to early literacy work.

There are a number of rhyming variations that you can work with. Here are a few examples:

> *Dad and Rod wandered round Hampstead.*

(End letters all rhyme.)

> *The dog and the frog went out in the fog.*

(Whole syllable rhyme in three words.)

Chicken Licken, Cyril Squirrel, Silly Billy.

(Examples of more than one syllable rhyming.)

Say these aloud, with children joining in, stressing the word endings to draw attention to them.

 Gradually children become phonologically aware of rhyming sounds in the middle of words, too.

When it's the vowel sounds that rhyme, it's called **assonance**.

When it's the consonant sounds that rhyme, or repeat, it's called **consonance**.

You can play oral word games anywhere and at any time.
They are ideal for when you have a quarter of an hour to fill!

> Examples of assonance:
> ... *blue moon mood* ...
> ... *Mum's coming up* ...
>
> Examples of consonance:
> ... *tittle tattle* ...
> ... *A short, sweet, story* ...

Many time-honoured nursery rhymes use a combination of all of these rhyming forms – alliteration, rhyme, consonance and assonance, which is why children who've been exposed to nursery rhymes generally have much better phonological awareness than those who haven't. This well-known rhyme is particularly rich:

> *Hickory Dickory Dock*
> *The mouse ran up the clock*
> *The clock struck one; the mouse ran down*
> *Hickory Dickory Dock.*

If you are working with children who are falling behind in their reading and who regard themselves as too old or too 'cool' for nursery rhymes, look out for short, funny, more 'grown-up' poems which do the same job. For example:

> *I always eat peas with honey*
> *I've done it all my life.*
> *They do taste kind of funny*
> *But it keeps them on the knife.*

(Sometimes wrongly attributed to Ogden Nash,
actually anonymous.)

Rhyming in the real world

 Look out for alliterative, rhyming, assonant and/or consonant football chants, advertising slogans and so on, which the children may be familiar with.

It's useful to keep a note of them all somewhere: you never know when they will prove useful.

 # Aiding whole-word recognition

Although whole-word approaches to teaching reading are currently not in favour, all reading depends to an extent on whole-word recognition. Certainly it's one of the tools that children use when they read.

It is sensible therefore to make it easier for children to build a sight vocabulary as their reading develops.

The main way that children do this is by recognising the shape of the word when it is written. So it's important that you do not destroy the outline shape of a word by writing for a child in block capitals. Capital letters make one word look very much like any other word of the same length.

> *Aeroplane*, with its 'p' partly below the line and its 'l' above, is visually much more distinctive than AEROPLANE.
>
> Similarly, *chimpanzee* is more instantly recognisable than CHIMPANZEE and *ambulance* than AMBULANCE.

It's for this reason, for example, that all road signs in the United Kingdom feature place names written in lower case letters – with initial capitals as necessary. It's much easier for drivers to 'read' a word written this way, as they approach the sign, than to read the same word written in block capitals. So it reduces the time spent reading road signs and increases the time spent concentrating on the road.

When you write for children who are learning to read, always use lower case letters, except where the rules dictate otherwise (e.g. for the initial letters of capitalised words such as names, the beginning of sentences, etc.).

2 Phonics Plus

2 Phonics Plus

The Issues

 ## Turning decoders into readers

Knowing your phonemes, your graphemes and your GPCs does not make you a reader. Similarly, being a good decoder of words and sentences does not make you a reader either.

A girl may be able to read whole strings of words in her decodable book quite accurately. But is she taking in what she is 'reading'? Is she understanding, or learning to understand, the meaning of the sentences? Are the words on the page being converted into stories, images or information in her head? Or is she, like a well-trained, rather bright dog, simply 'barking at print' – recognising the words and obediently saying them aloud, without really reading (in the full sense) at all?

 Never lose sight of the simple fact that children learn phonics in order to be able to read.

They don't read in order to prove their phonics ability.

There is a big difference between reading and barking at print.

You only become a reader by reading. There's no stage when you can say 'I can read, so I can stop now.' A reader is somebody who reads, not somebody who used to read.

Not only must children be taught how to decode words and sentences, they must also constantly be encouraged to use the skills they're acquiring.

That means that children need to read as often as possible. They need to read books, captions, football league tables, jokes, emails, the school lunch menu, text messages on a mobile phone and anything else which is written and which the child is interested in.

Research by Wray and Medwell in 1999* found that the most effective teachers of literacy put decoding skills into context by using meaningful texts (meaningful to the reader, that is) for real purposes.

*What makes an effective teacher of literacy? David Wray and Jane Medwell, University of Warwick, published in Literacy Today June 1999.

 Remember, every child is interested in something.

Otherwise there is a danger that children will see reading as something very difficult that they are forced to pit themselves against in school, but which is not relevant to their 'real' life.

So reading has to be presented not only as a piece of mechanical learning, but also as an activity which has a context – such as a story a child really wants to read, an account of last night's football match, a paragraph about someone the child has seen on television, or whatever.

What this all boils down to is that you need regular practice. You only learn to read – *really* read – by reading.

That way you gradually become a more confident reader and you can keep going for longer without flagging. You build what the experts call reading stamina.

Synthetic phonics plus

The pendulum has swung firmly in favour of synthetic phonics in recent years but, as we've seen, that doesn't mean that other approaches are no longer relevant.

 Remember the story of the blind man and the elephant? He tried to identify the animal by touch. Feeling the shape of its trunk, he thought it was a snake; feeling its leg he thought it was a tree. Only when he had put the big picture together was he able to identify the elephant for what it was.

Learning to read is just the same.

It's true that the various approaches we've already discussed – whole-word/sight vocabulary, flashcards, real books and analytic phonics – all have too many shortcomings to be used as the primary (i.e. main) method for teaching children to read; but that is far from saying that these approaches have no value.

Synthetic phonics brings a rigour and a method to tackling texts: it gives children strategies to recognise unfamiliar words, thus reducing guesswork.

It is right that synthetic phonics should, for the majority of children, form the basis of literacy teaching.

Analytic phonics can bring quick fixes to decoding more complex words such as *thinking (th - ink - ing)*. And a sight vocabulary facilitates more fluent reading.

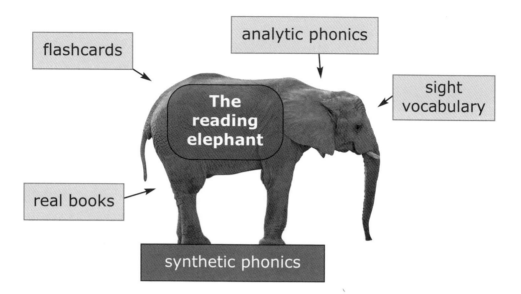

Yet each of the approaches we've discussed – including synthetic phonics – will, on its own, only get the child so far down the road to reading.

As in all things, it's a question of balance. Children need context for their reading and lots of opportunities to practise it in an enjoyable, informative and useful way. But they also need to acquire decoding skills in a systematic way, because it offers a sound basis for approaching everything else.

> Real reading success comes when you, the teacher, are able to help the child put together the best of each approach to read fluently and with pleasure.

 ## Building 'the house of literacy'

Compare synthetic phonics with the foundations of a large building. Without good foundations the building will collapse and fall down. On the other hand, there is a great deal more to any building than its foundations (which, after all, are usually invisible so that we're not conscious of them). What we see in a building are its rooms, its space and style.

W hen we help children build their houses of literacy, we must put solid foundations in place for them. Synthetic phonics offers the most effective way of building these foundations.

But equally, there is a great deal more to our house of literacy than its foundations. Being able to read books, notices, timetables, the Internet and sources of information of all sorts and in all formats – fluently – requires more than just an understanding of synthetic phonics.

In favour of mixed methods

 When children read, as we have seen, they use a variety of methods (whether we introduce them all or not). We cannot (and

Reading is a pleasure. But it requires practice, fluency and stamina.

should not) forbid emergent readers from taking help in the way they find it.

For example, opponents of 'mixed methods' (who usually want nothing but synthetic phonics to be used) loathe this approach because they say that it relies partly on guesswork.

Well yes, it does – and it has to. Cast your mind back. How did you cope with strange words such as *annihilate*, *vehement* and *brougham* when you first met them in print? The fact is, you would not have known how to pronounce them until someone told you or you heard them spoken.

And if you are reading an illustrated book – say on a science topic – and you meet a word you don't know, do you refer to the accompanying illustrations to help you work out what the word might mean? Of course you do. You'd be foolish not to. Should we therefore prevent children from looking at the illustrations in their reading books? Some teachers and specialists argue (wrongly in my view) that we should.

② Synthetic phonics does not suit all children.

Some children, for whatever reason, fail to learn to read fluently with phonics in their early years.

So teachers and other adults have to find other ways of helping to build up these children's literacy, as they progress through primary school and into secondary education.

③ Phonics does not help with irregular words – words that are not phonetically decodable. Take, for example, that well-known group of stumbling blocks: *plough*, *dough*, *tough*, *through*, *cough* and *borough*.

I had a friend at school called Marian Hough. How do you pronounce her surname? We spent years listening to new teachers guessing – amusing for us but tiresome for poor Marian. In fact it rhymed with *cough*, but there were at least five other possibilities. You learn to read such words only by guessing, being helped and then committing them to memory.

2 Phonics Plus

Practical Teaching Ideas

The strategies that follow are all aimed at making children and young people more 'reading aware', or at starting them on the first rungs of the reading ladder. These strategies can easily be adapted to the age group you are working with, and so can be used with early years children, as well as in getting much older pupils on track with their reading.

Parents can do a lot of this at home too. The advantage of doing it at home, of course, is that 'home' isn't 'school' and therefore it can't be 'work'.

Stories

Reading with the child

✐ When you read a book to, or with, a child make sure you can both see the pages of the book. (Someone once said that the very best children's book was big enough to spread across two laps.) This applies to parents and teachers, whether reading with their children at home or at school.

✐ Run your finger lightly along the print as you read the words, to draw the child's attention to it. As the child's sight vocabulary (i.e. words they know and can recognise without sounding them out) develops, stop at the occasional word and let them read it – but keep the flow of the sentence going, so that you don't lose the narrative pulse.

If it's a book they are familiar with, such as one of David McKee's *Elmer the Elephant* books, you might get them to read the word *Elmer*, or *Elephant*, every time you come to it.

✐ Gradually you can increase the number of words they read and decrease the number that you read.

This is where (for parents) it's very useful to know the stage that your child has reached in their reading at school. If you know which phonemes your child has covered, for example, you can quickly work out which words in the book you can ask them to read. You will also be more confident in your requests: 'You should be able to read this word,' or 'This one's hard, but see if you can do it ...'

Teachers, please note: many parents are very keen to help their children read at home, but they are often not sure what exactly they can do to help.

Parents and carers at home are effectively free sources of teaching support – but you need to give them some direction about how best to help. So keep parents in the loop.

And never underestimate the damage that a misdirected 'pushy' parent can do to a child's attitude to reading – not to mention their self-esteem.

Reading stories aloud

> Experiencing stories is the single most important factor in eventually learning to read. Every child should hear several stories every day.

It is vital that children see books in use and learn that good things come out of them. But they also need the communication skills that come from listening to – and watching the face of – a story *teller*, as opposed to a story *reader*.

✎ Pointing to the words on the page as you read them gets the children used to the idea – or reminds them – that print has *meaning*. They will gradually start to recognise some of the word shapes. If they hear the same story often enough, some will learn it by heart and then 'read' it to themselves or to toys, often turning the pages at the right time. This is a good sign that the child is on the way to literacy.

> But the converse isn't necessarily true. If a child doesn't do this, it doesn't mean that they aren't on the way to literacy. So don't panic. Remember, all children are different.

✎ If you are reading a story to young children from a book, sit with the child or children, so that the text and the illustrations are visible to both (or all) of you.

✎ Point to the words as you read them. Don't be afraid to make up extra bits to enrich the story.

If you do depart from the written text, and if the child is 'reading' along with you, then let the child know that you are not always following the text – otherwise they will get lost and lose any reading confidence they have built up.

Point to the words as you read to the child.

 With very young children, you might base your story on a toy – '*Here's Bertie the Bunny and he's going to find some carrots to eat. Look, here he goes ...*'

If you are telling a story, make it as dramatic as you can, with lots of gestures and eye contact. Digress (at appropriate moments) to tell the children about things that have happened to you in real life.

 Large format books, often known as 'big books' and produced by several publishers, are good for using with large groups or whole classes of children from age 5 to 8 or 9.

Reading with older children

However hard-bitten and 'cool' youngsters think they are, almost all will listen to a good story read aloud. Many years ago, when I was teaching 'difficult' secondary school boys in London, most of whom had very low reading levels, I used to read aloud to them as a way of getting control and getting their attention – but it had many other longer term benefits too!

✍ With older children, tap into their own interests, such as football. If you were present at a famous match (for example, a Cup Final), tell them about it. And most youngsters love tales of the teachers' own childhood.

For older children, tapping into *their* interests (such as computer games or fly fishing), whilst making it obvious that you recognise that these are clearly not the interests of younger children, sends a clear signal that you are sensitive to the reader as an individual, and not just teaching 'by rote'.

> The best story I ever found for Years 5, 6 and 7 (ages 9 – 14) is *Spit Nolan* by Bill Naughton. Another wonderful one for the same age group is *The Christmas Gift* by Hugh Oliver, which is in *An Oxford Book of Christmas Stories* (1986).

 Many publishers now offer non-fiction titles on high interest-age topics for older, struggling readers. In many cases the text is set at a lower reading age level, which offers an ideal entry point for text-averse reluctant readers.

Killer Plants and Body Art. Two high interest-age titles for struggling readers. Part of the Trailblazers series, from Ransom Publishing.

✏ Don't be afraid to read aloud snippets from magazines, newspapers, comics and websites that are likely to interest them. Some children (especially boys) develop an aversion to books. So reading things that aren't books neatly circumvents that resistance. It also shows poor readers the value of reading – something that is often not emphasised enough.

Around and about: harnessing visual literacy

Children learn to 'read' visual symbols, logos, pictures and so on long before they can decode words. I was recently driving a child of two years and 20 months up the A10 towards Cambridge. I stopped at a Tesco superstore so that we could both use the toilets. As soon as we got out of the car, the child looked up and said 'Oh it's Tesco!' – even though she had never been to this branch before. Without knowing a single letter or phonetic sound, and way off reading print, she had 'read' the familiar, distinctive red and blue Tesco logo.

When you are teaching a child to read – irrespective of age – it makes sense to use this visual literacy: 'Yes, it's Tesco. Look, it starts with a /t/.'

> You can also do a lot by looking at pictures with children and encouraging them to talk and make up stories about them.

Collecting pictures

✏ Collect interesting pictures. These can then be used as cues for reading and writing about the world around us. Magazine and newspaper colour supplements (especially advertisements) are a useful source of pictures. Have heaps of them in the classroom, so that pupils can look through them to find pictures too. Just use each picture once or twice and then throw them away when they get tatty. It is very easy to find more.

✏ Mix the mundane (e.g. pictures of local shops and buildings) with the exotic (e.g. pictures from space, or pictures from distant countries). Also look for dramatic pictures, such as people pulling faces or standing in unusual places. Adverts often feature animals or cars in unlikely situations. Pictures of houses are good too. So are sports shots and 'cool' cars.

Every picture tells a story. What stories do these pictures tell?

'Talk-about' pictures

✏ A variation is to collect 'talk about' pictures – often photographs taken by you or by someone else in school, or copyright-free images from the Internet (check this carefully) – and show them to children on an electronic whiteboard.

✏ Talk to the children about one of the pictures. Depending on their age, ask them simple questions about it. 'What do you think this lady's doing?' 'What is she waiting for?' 'What is she going to do next?' And so on.

✏ You can also move on to other things that might be happening beyond the picture. (Are her children waiting to be picked up from school in that car? What are the children's names? Where will they sit?) If a person is pulling a face, what are they frightened of, or laughing at?

> Gradually draw a 'back story' from the children to go with the picture. This could be done with an emphasis on veracity, or it could be done as a pure fantasy exercise – in which case encourage the children to be as creative as possible with their ideas.

Then later a child with whom an adult has been working one-to-one might be able to tell a classmate everything that they and you have imagined about the picture. In other words, they may be able to recount the story to someone else. It will probably come out with even more embellishments, but that's all to the good!

Logos

Another way of harnessing visual literacy is to play a guessing game with logos. Collect logos from advertisements – for cars, computer games, trainers and so on – and ask the children to say which product each logo belongs too. If nothing else, it proves to the child that, in a sense, they can read.

Making notices

Whether you are at home or at school, make notices (or labels) and attach them to furniture and other items around you. The children can help you do this.

Many of these notices (*cupboard, nature corner, photograph*) are not phonetic and need to be learned as whole words. With others which are phonetic (*chair, tray, bed*), it is still useful reinforcement for the child to see them displayed. But remember not to write them in upper case (block capital) letters. Use lower case letters so that the words retain a distinctive shape.

Group games

Making up stories in groups

Another way of experiencing stories is by inventing them together. You can make this into a game that develops confidence, language use, oral skills and imagination. It also encourages listening – all of which are essential to the development of literacy.

✎ Sit in a circle with a group of children. Start to tell a very simple story. For example:

> *'Once upon a time there was a boy named James. He lived in a house near the park with his mum, dad and a dog called Bill.*
>
> *One day ...'*

✎ Stop and ask the child next to you to go on. When they have added a bit, move on to the next child and so on. Continue round the circle, letting the story build up. Inevitably in the end it will get (very?) silly and you can all laugh about it.

✎ Then you can start again. As soon as the children get the hang of the game, you can get one of them to start, rather than starting it yourself. However you might like to go on taking a turn as the story comes round, so that you can steer it or keep it going.

✎ For even more fun: as they get better at it, limit them to one word each – so that they have to build the sentences by batting the words around the circle, like a game of pass the parcel. It forces the children to concentrate, and they have to think about how words fit together – all grist to the reading mill!

O ne of the useful things about this game is that, because all narrative is sentence-based, players quite quickly grasp the sense of what a sentence is. So in time you might limit them to one sentence each.

'I spy' with phonics

'I spy' is a good old spelling favourite, but it can be adapted to be played with young pupils long before they can visualise how words are written. It encourages children to listen to spoken words and think about the sounds that they begin with.

 Working with a group of four or five children, begin by saying 'I spy with my little eye something beginning with [*say*] /*c*/.' Use the phonetic sound rather than the alphabet letter name (i.e. /*c*/ as in *cat*, not as in *centre*).

Choose items in the room that begin with a pure, hard /*c*/ sound (*carrot*, *cat*, *cupboard*, *coat*). Don't use items which happen to be spelt with a 'c' but which begin with a different sound (*ceiling*, *circle*). At this stage avoid words like *Christmas tree*, and avoid consonant blends (*crayon*, *cloth*) too.

> So if it's /*t*/, for example, stick to *toy*, *table* or *timer*, not *tray*, *thorn* or *throat*.

Then let the children try to guess the word that you are thinking of. The child who gets the right answer is the next person to say 'I spy ...'

Once the children are secure with single letter sounds, you can move on to playing the game with sounds made by two or even three letters (consonant blends), such as *bridge*, *bread* and *brick*, or *drink*, *drum* and *dragon*, or *string*, *strong* and *strap*. 'I spy with my little eye something beginning with /*dr*/.'

 Other phonemes which work well with this game are /*bl*/, /*cl*/, /*fl*/, /*fr*/, /*gr*/, /*gl*/, /*pl*/, /*pr*/, /*sl*/ and /*shr*/.

'I spy' for older children

Older children might find the version of 'I spy' described above too 'babyish.' But there are ways around this.

 Put one older 'responsible' child (i.e. a child who needs the phonic practice) in charge of organising the game, with a group of younger children from a different class.

 Play the game with the names of football players (or other sports personalities), or sports teams.

> 'I can think of a player whose names begin with /*w*/ and /*r*/.' Or: 'I can think of a team beginning with /*s*/ and /*w*/ or /*w*/ and /*w*/.'
> (Wayne Rooney, Sheffield Wednesday and Wolverhampton Wanderers respectively).

To help, you could have a list of teams and players displayed on the classroom wall, or on an electronic whiteboard.

 Do something similar with pop stars, or characters from TV soaps.

'Relax and enjoy' word games

Success in literacy requires getting away from the heavy, anxious 'We've got to get you reading or else ...' approach and cultivating a more 'laid back' manner.

Group literacy games are fun – and they build confidence, too.

lways make word and letter work fun. Playing with words helps children absorb the links between sounds and letters. So the more word games you have at your disposal, the better.

Here, for example is a silly – and very simple – game which reminds or teaches children to hear and be aware of the sounds that words start with.

The idea is to find alliterative names for animals.

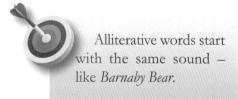

Alliterative words start with the same sound – like *Barnaby Bear*.

So you might start with *Felix Fox*. With some prompting – and probably a lot of laughter – you and the pupils will think of lots more names, such as: *Henry Hare, Katie Kangaroo* and *Zach Zebra*. The sillier the names, the more fun it is (*Abdullah Anteater, Yasmin Yak, Eric Elephant*). You could try finding one for every letter of the alphabet.

> The next stage could be to build the animal name into an alliterative sentence – such as *Felicity Fox fought furiously,* or *Henry Hare hurried home.*

 And if literacy-weary older children think this is just too silly (too silly for words?!), ask them to draw/paint/create on a computer the creatures that they have named – for younger children in the school. Each illustration should have the appropriate name (e.g. *Ryan Rabbit*) written beneath it. They could even create a splendid new alphabet frieze for the children in Reception Year.

 If, for the sake of the older children, you need to make one further step towards 'cool', you could ask them to create alliterative names for 'mythical' creatures in a Pokemon-style computer game.

The Doctor's Dog

Here's another old favourite – but it may be new to your children. It's a game called *The Doctor's Dog* and it extends vocabulary, encourages concentration and helps with alphabet knowledge.

 In a group of two, three or four, the first player (perhaps yourself?) says, for example, 'The doctor's dog is an *active* dog'. The second player says 'The doctor's dog is an *awful* dog', and the third 'The doctor's dog is an *amazing* dog' – and so on, until everyone in the group has had a turn with adjectives beginning with 'a' to describe the dog.

Then start the next round with 'b': 'The doctor's dog is a *brown* dog.' 'The doctor's dog is a *beautiful* dog.' 'The doctor's dog is a *bad* dog' ... and so on. Repeat the rounds until every player has had a turn with every letter of the alphabet. It gets quite challenging if you're the fourth person to get 'x'! Make sure everyone says the whole sentence each time – because it has a fluent rhythm (and it's quite funny).

 An older version of this game began with 'The parson's cat ...', but nowadays children are unlikely to know what a parson is. So think of new variations such as 'The postman's parrot ...' or 'The caretaker's cat ...' . Or use a name with an animal, such as Hari's hamster ... Mum's mouse ... or Sangita's snake ... .

You can play this game anywhere because it needs no equipment, so it's a useful one for the dinner queue or on the coach en route for football practice.

But don't mention 'literacy' – just suggest it as a bit of fun to fill the time.

Beginnings and endings

Being able to hear the component sounds that make up words is essential if you are going to be able to read and write them.

There is not enough emphasis on listening in most literacy teaching. Many children spell words incorrectly simply because they don't hear them spoken correctly.

So, in this noisy world which throws a 24/7 cacophony of sounds at our youngsters, we need to find ways of helping them to *listen* and *hear* (not quite the same thing) attentively and selectively.

Obviously, if you are trying to develop reading, you will habitually stress the opening sounds of words (what in analytic phonics is called the **onset**) and the children will soon learn to hear and recognise them.

Then it's time to encourage them to tune into end sounds as well (in analytic phonics, the **rime**).

That involves developing an understanding that words can begin with the same letters that others end with.

 Play a game in which you get the children to build chains of words where each word starts with the sound the previous one ended with.

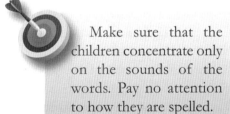 For example: *kitchen – name – mouse – song.*

When you come to the end of a chain, start another one, such as *football – league – goal – leather* and so on. Try getting the children to take turns to think of the next link in the chain, or 'brainstorm' it together as a group.

 When the group is ready to take this further, try playing the game visually (i.e. using written words) rather than orally. The children can then look at the last letter and try to think of another word beginning with that letter. This helps both reading and spelling.

Make sure that the children concentrate only on the sounds of the words. Pay no attention to how they are spelled.

To play the game visually, you will need to write the words on a flipchart or whiteboard as you go. Alternatively, you (or the children) could build the words using letter tiles.

Note that, as children can think of any word (and not just phonetically decodable words), they may need some guidance in getting the correct spellings of any difficult words.

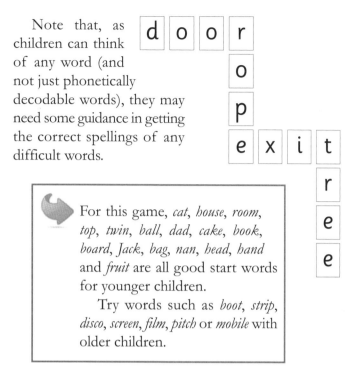

> For this game, *cat, house, room, top, twin, ball, dad, cake, book, board, Jack, bag, nan, head, hand* and *fruit* are all good start words for younger children.
>
> Try words such as *boot, strip, disco, screen, film, pitch* or *mobile* with older children.

Letter games

Word-building

At an early stage of learning to read and write, it is common to use letter bricks, magnetic letters, or tiles to build words. This is good practice because it increases knowledge of the correspondence between letters and sounds – the first step in creating words. Magnetic letters – the sort you might stick on a fridge door – are particularly good to work with. Most sets come with a metal board.

 Make simple three-letter words by moving the bricks or tiles.

> For example, say to a child: 'Can you find a /*m*/?'
> Then 'Let's put /*a*/ next to it and then /*n*/.'
> (Make sure you use the letter sounds, not the
> letter names, throughout.)
> Finally you say: 'Look, we've made *man*.'

Encourage the children to move the letters around and work out/sound out any new words they've made.

> So if you change the 'm' in *man* to a 'p', it becomes
> *pan*. If you change the 'n' at the end to a 'p' it
> becomes *map*. If you change the 'a' in the middle
> to an 'e' it makes *men*.

Encourage the children to experiment with the combinations. *Bag* is another good base word. So is *pip*. It doesn't matter much if some of the words the children suggest are 'made up' (such as *vot, yag* or *mip*). You are still building up literacy skills.

As the children progress, move on to making words using combined letters (consonant blends and digraphs) such as /*br*/, /*cl*/, /*dr*/, /*sh*/ and so on.

The more closely this is tied to the synthetic phonics programme the child is following at school, the better the learning will be embedded.

 ## Word-building with older children

If you're working with an older group, bricks and tiles could seem like a babyish turn-off. 'Grown-up' alternatives to bricks or tiles include:

- Putting random letters on a computer screen and encouraging the child/student to mouse-drag them into words.

- Getting the children to cut letters from the headlines in 'grown-up' newspapers and gum them onto paper to make words (this encourages motor skills, such as the use of scissors and application of gum, too). This is a fiddly activity which will appeal to a certain type of child.

  It's also an activity which could be developed as a 'Ransom note' theme.

I need Help. Can you find me?

- Scrabble tiles. Working with tiles from the popular 'Scrabble' game means that the children are effectively playing a version of a 'grown-up' game. You could even make use of the score count on each tile – that offers an incentive to use the less common letters and includes a bit of numeracy work as a bonus.

Alphabet-learning games

As well as learning the phonetic sounds that letters make (or combine to make) in words, readers also need to know the alphabet (in order) by letter names (i.e. 'ay', 'bee', 'see' rather than 'ah', 'buh', 'cuh'). Without this knowledge they will never be able to use a dictionary or an index, or to spell a word aloud.

- With young children, a good way of teaching the alphabet is by means of the alphabet song. There are several well-known versions. Sing it with the group several times, until they begin to pick it up. With older children who are past such 'childish' activities (but who still do not know the alphabet), try fitting it to a more grown-up tune, such as the latest pop song or sports chant.

- Play a game using the alphabet song as an interlude. To begin, a child has to think of the name of an animal. After they have said it aloud, everyone sings the alphabet song to give the next child time to think of another animal. You can probably go round the circle several times, by which time everyone will probably be quite confident with the alphabet.

You can, of course, vary the game by using some other 'commodity' such as fruits, flowers, sports, foods or whatever, rather than just animals.

Make sure you have the alphabet – with both upper and lower case for each letter – displayed somewhere in the classroom.

If you happen also to be trying to develop basic computer keyboard skills, get them to type the alphabet using word processing software.

Hold a competition. Give a small prize to the child who can type the alphabet accurately the fastest. Get them to monitor their own speeds with a stopwatch, so that they have an incentive to beat their own time.

3 Helping Strugglers

3 Helping Strugglers

 The Issues

 Literacy is an essential life skill

Whatever teaching methods are used, it seems to be the case that some children forge ahead with their reading and writing, whilst others tend to get left behind. This shouldn't be surprising: in any human endeavour, there are those who do very well, and there are those who struggle.

But reading is different. Unlike horse-riding, acting, plate-spinning (or many other human activities) the ability to read is an essential skill.

> An adult who cannot read will find it very difficult to shop in supermarkets, read a manual for a simple household appliance, use a computer, or look up a plumber in the Yellow Pages when the water pipes burst.

It's imperative therefore that we find ways to support those children who find reading difficult and who fail to get to grips with it.

An important tool in measuring a child's reading ability is the idea of the 'reading age'. There are various tests to ascertain a child's reading age, although many of them are quite crude. Nevertheless, the principle stands: an *average* child will have a reading age that is the same as their actual, or chronological, age. So an average eight year-old will have a reading age of eight.

Now, obviously, since not all children conform to the average, some children will have a reading age above their actual age, and for others it will be lower than their actual age. The actual spread follows the familiar Bell curve.

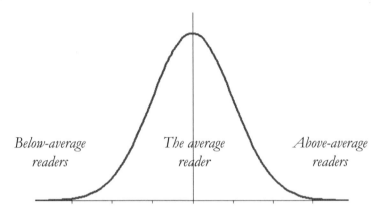

Below-average readers *The average reader* *Above-average readers*

The Bell curve

 So, for example, a very competent reader, aged seven, might be tested and considered to have a reading age of ten.

Children who are reading above their actual age do not present a problem. (In fact, they *do* present a problem – but of a different kind. It is often difficult to find age-appropriate books for them to read.)

However a child who is reading below their actual age – say a ten year-old with a reading age of six – needs specific help to improve their reading and writing.

Reluctant and struggling readers

Children with a reading age below (or substantially below) their chronological age (also sometimes – and more usefully – described as their interest age) are commonly referred to as struggling readers.

But there are also children who can read perfectly well (they are close to average or above average in terms of their reading levels) but who are reluctant to do so.

For whatever reason, they have never acquired the habit of reading and they don't enjoy reading books.

Reluctance to read is a common issue with boys in particular, and teachers often complain that they are told that 'books are boring'.

So it is important to distinguish between reluctant readers – where the problem is engaging interest – and struggling readers, who are readers with a low reading age relative to their actual age, and who may still be having trouble with simple decoding.

I hope I've convinced you earlier in this book that reading successfully is not just about being able to decode the squiggles on a page and turn them into words. Building the 'house of literacy' involves much more than just being able to decode print.

For this reason, we should continue to be concerned about reluctant readers – children who *can* read but don't. It is important that we continue to try to find ways to engage them with text (not necessarily with books), as they need to continue to develop their vocabulary and their reading stamina.

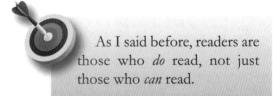

As I said before, readers are those who *do* read, not just those who *can* read.

Having said that, my primary focus in this chapter is on ways to help struggling readers.

Helping struggling readers

Some children who are struggling with reading really do want to read, and look forward to sitting down with a good book – even though they find the process of reading it difficult. Notwithstanding, I think it's fair to say that most struggling readers don't enjoy reading. They find it hard work, they find it unrewarding, and it's not something they look forward to.

In that regard, struggling readers share many characteristics with reluctant readers: they don't enjoy it, they find books boring and they will usually seek out other activities in preference to reading a book. None of this should be surprising. When reading is hard work it ceases to be a pleasure.

Struggling readers very commonly become reluctant readers.

However, our struggling reader's reluctance to read is overlaid with a number of other issues which make it a tricky problem to tackle.

1 **Disengagement**. A child is not going to develop an enthusiasm for reading if reading itself is so difficult and unrewarding all the time. Failure is not a great motivator.

2 **Low self-esteem**. Few things are more demoralising than being made to go back to the beginning of something because you haven't 'got it'. And all the time the child is getting older, so the activities seem more and more babyish. Struggling readers often describe themselves as failures.

3 **Feelings of inevitability**. '*I couldn't do it last time, or the time before that, so why should this time be any different?*'

Each time the child struggles unsuccessfully with a passage of text is, in their eyes, further 'proof' that they cannot read. In other words, their feeling that failure is inevitable is reinforced by their further failure. This in turn feeds their low self-esteem, which in turn feeds their disengagement from reading ... which starts the whole vicious cycle all over again.

4 **Lack of age-appropriate books**. A twelve year-old boy with a reading age of (say) seven is not going to be very happy reading a book designed for a seven year-old. It's going to be too babyish in terms of style and content. But a book designed for a twelve year-old is going to be too difficult for our struggling reader to read.

The solution of course lies in finding books that have the right interest age (in this case, twelve) and the right reading age (in this case seven). Thankfully a number of publishers now specialise in publishing this kind of 'high interest-age, low reading-age', or 'high-low' books.

Ransom Publishing and *Barrington Stoke* are two of the best-known publishers of high-low books of this type.

The 'Dark Man' series of books, published by Ransom Publishing, have an interest age of around fourteen and up, with a very low reading age (starting at around six years).

Notwithstanding the efforts of these specialist publishers, there is still a general shortage of age-appropriate books for struggling readers. After all, finding the right book involves getting both the interest age and the reading age right, and then finding the topic or topics that appeal to each of our struggling, reluctant readers.

Helping struggling readers first of all involves making key interventions to break the negative cycle of failure, low self-esteem and disengagement.

What struggling readers badly need are some successes, however small, to build some confidence and self-belief.

So the first challenge is to find fresh ways of starting again, without it seeming too infantile.

> It's one thing to teach literacy to very young children, but quite a different challenge to do it with older children. It requires tact and ingenuity.

This is made more difficult since an older struggling reader has already been exposed to a few years of (relatively unsuccessful) teaching. Issues of motivation aside, they may well have picked up bad habits over this period – for example using whole-word approaches to reading rather than phonics-based approaches, or they may be confusing the letters 'b' and 'd' (a common problem).

Working with older struggling readers often requires unpicking bad habits as much as revisiting first principles.

So let's move on to look at some practical approaches.

3 Helping Strugglers

Practical Teaching Ideas

 ## Developing listening skills

When working with struggling readers, you may need to go back to the very beginning and focus on listening skills. This is because children – whatever their age – won't be able to hear phonemes in words until they have learned to distinguish sounds. So here are some suggestions for developing listening skills in older readers.

 ### Drama and rhyme

✐ Devise some imaginative sound-focused drama activities. Make sure that they don't come across as 'literacy' or 'reading'. Get the children to make sounds for surprise ('Ooooooo!') appreciation ('Mmmmm!'), not fair ('Aaaaah!') and so on.

✐ Create an activity that involves the children completing a rhyming statement. This helps tune their ears for rhyming

sounds. Emphasise that they should focus on the sounds they hear, rather than on the spellings of the words.

> For example, you say
> 'Who gave the pearl to the ... ?'
>
> (answer: *girl*),
>
> or 'Guy flew very ... '
>
> (answer: *high*),
>
> or 'This is the man whom Carrie will ... '
>
> (answer: *marry*),
>
> or 'Paul kicked the ... '
>
> (answer: *ball*).

✐ You can also get the children to make these rhyming statements up for each other. Again, make sure they ignore spellings altogether and focus only on sounds.

Using pictures

✐ Assemble a number of pictures of various objects (cut out from magazines or comics, etc.). Then get the children to sort the pictures into piles, according to the letter with which each object pictured begins. Choose pictures that are likely to appeal to the age group – so footballers and lip gloss are probably preferable to teddy bears and trains.

Raps and songs

✐ Raps are always a good activity, especially for older boys. (Raps are often very acceptable to children who would refuse to do the same if it was called poetry). Raps emphasise both rhythm and rhyme, and it is quite easy for children to make up raps of their own.

✐ If you are short of subject matter for your raps, you can always begin by asking the children to make up their own raps celebrating

Karaoke is a great activity for older strugglers.

somebody's birthday, or a recent sports victory (e.g. by the school team, or their favourite football team).

- Some children like 'songs from the shows' too – and they're full of words and rhythm (think of *The Lonely Goatherd* from *The Sound of Music*). So, oddly, are some songs by Elvis Presley – the 'King' had remarkably clear diction! Try a sing-along with close attention to the words.

- Keep your ears tuned to the latest pop hits and to favourite television programmes. Are there any songs that can be used in the classroom as a starting point for listening activities?

- Another alternative is to organise a karaoke competition, using (for example) pop videos from YouTube (*www.youtube.com*). Many pop music favourites have been uploaded to YouTube as karaoke-ready versions, with the words presented on-screen as part of the video. A perfect listening (and reading) opportunity!

✏️ You can also make a game of clapping, stamping or finger clicking the rhythm in words such as *Oliver*, *Everton* or *Elizabeth*. Again, this can be extended to the names of sports stars, TV stars or pop stars.

✏️ And do anything else you can think of with music and sounds, appropriate to the age group, to develop attentive listening. That is then a 'music lesson' not 'reading' or 'literacy.'

Tapping into what the child can 'read' already

Even children who are not 'taking to' reading often learn to recognise words and letters in the context of things they're interested in. Equally, many children 'read' letters and words that they meet in their everyday life – on street signs, or in shop windows. It's as if their curiosity drives them to want to understand – and, as this isn't 'reading' as they know it, they aren't resistant to it.

My elder son, for example – whose name happens to be Lucas – noticed very early in life that his name appeared on most car headlights (which, when he was about three, were at his eye-level). And think of the non-reading older boy whom we met in Chapter One, who could find the words *Tyrannosaurus Rex* in a book.

You can use this body of acquired reading knowledge as a starting point to develop their literacy further, without imposing 'reading' (i.e. using books).

Here are some ideas along these lines.

 ## Road signs, street signs

✏️ Make the most of road signs – the signs that have place names and other writing on them, as well as the standard signs (such as 'No Entry') which we read via a shape or symbol. Even a struggling reader will already be able to 'read' some of these, so it's a quick success that's good for self-esteem.

Road signs offer good reading opportunities.

✏ Take photographs of local signs and use them in school on an electronic whiteboard or ordinary computer screen. Don't limit this to road signs. Photograph the names of familiar shops, advertising hoardings, 'For sale' signs and even the names on the backs of cars. This is all very easy to do with a digital camera. If you are a parent, you can do this when you are 'out and about' with your children.

✏ Encourage the children to tell you and each other what the signs say or mean.

Point out what skilled 'readers' they actually are – building confidence as you go.

Talk to, and with, them about the purposes of road signs. Get them to design and draw their own signs, advertisements and/or names for cars. They might then make maps of the area, with the streets and important buildings labelled.

Sports (again!)

 For children who are keen on football or any other sports (and that probably includes most boys), look at the professional league tables for that sport. You can access them via the Internet. You could display the league tables on an electronic whiteboard. What do the tables show? Many children will already know where their team is and which teams are in the same division – so now look at the words and get them to read them with you.

You'll find comprehensive, up-to-date league tables on the BBC Sport website, for example, at *news.bbc.co.uk/sport*.

The names of many football teams have a wonderful poetic rhythm.

> For example, *West Bromwich Albion* is a series of three words, each with one syllable more than the one before. In each case the first syllable is stressed.
>
> The two words in *Sheffield Wednesday* share the same first vowel sound, so they are assonant. *Wolverhampton Wanderers*, with its two /w/ onset sounds, is alliterative.

Of course you don't need to go into these technicalities with the children, but be aware that it's why they enjoy saying them and why football results read aloud sound like a poem.

Can you and your pupils write a poem using the names of the football teams they support?

Anything which gets them to focus on words is helping to develop their reading.

Using appropriate reading matter

An older child who is, for whatever reason, falling behind in reading will be turned off by books full of twee talking animals that are written for four year-olds.

So, to generate or maintain motivation, you need to find easy-to-read books – both fiction and non-fiction – which have the right interest level.

However, getting the reading age and the interest age right is only the first step. The books will also need to be on the right topics, presented in the right way.

If you're going to motivate a disengaged reader to want to read, you'll need to find a topic they are interested in.

In terms of generating enthusiasm and then carrying this momentum through in reading, the question you need to ask yourself is always the same: 'What's in it for them?'

Think about it. *You* are probably selective about what books you read. Why shouldn't a (non-reading) child also be choosy?

Motivation is key.

 ## Educational books

 As I've already mentioned, a number of publishers are now aware of this need, and publish ranges of high interest-age, low reading-age (or 'high-low') books.

✏ Ransom Publishing has made a speciality of this area, with series such as *Boffin Boy* (by David Orme) and *Dark Man* (by Peter Lancett). Both series have reading ages of 6 – 7, with higher interest ages. There are also accompanying workbooks for these series.

(*The Dark Man* series of books, shown on page 74, is designed to appeal to teenagers and young adults. Despite the very low reading ages, these books are not suitable for the under twelves).

The 'Boffin Boy' series of books, published by Ransom Publishing. The comic format makes the books appear less educational – although the text is carefully levelled to a specific reading age.

Ransom's *Trailblazers* series similarly presents non-fiction topics (each with both non-fiction and a 500 word fiction story included).

See *www.ransom.co.uk* for details of these and other high-low series.

✏ Nelson Thornes has a series called *Fast Lane*, in which the content is kept to a low (graded) reading level, but is aimed at the interests of older children. *Shipwreck*, for example, has 981 words and is an adventure story set out like a comic strip. Frequently-used words and phonic opportunities are pointed out to the teacher inside the front cover. The series has 142 titles at 20 different levels and includes both fiction and non-fiction.

Each *Fast Lane* book comes with a mini CD in a pocket on the front. The CD for *Shipwreck* has the story clearly narrated and partly dramatised by three voices. In other instances the content is read by a single voice.

Other books and resources

🖎 The advantage of using books published by educational publishers is obvious: you can be confident that the text has been carefully written and levelled for a specific reading age, to ensure that the reader does not meet any unduly difficult words.

However there is no reason why you cannot use other books and resources, provided that you exercise care in how they are selected.

🖎 The advantage of using 'non-educational' books and magazines, etc. is that you might be able to tap directly into an individual child's passions – whether it be a favourite movie, television programme (e.g. Top Gear or Doctor Who) or computer game. It can make their reading seem worthwhile.

> Most high-profile TV programmes and movies have associated comics, magazines, books and/or websites to support the brand. These can all be used to help engage and motivate the child in their reading.

Audio-books

Audio-books (i.e. narrated versions of the books) are a great way to introduce children to stories – specifically, to narratives that don't involve associated moving pictures!

Audio-books are especially useful for older children who may find it embarrassing to have an adult (or another child) read to them.

🖎 Many audio-books can now be purchased on CD or downloaded from the Internet, and these offer a great starting point.

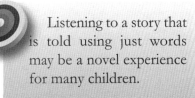

Listening to a story that is told using just words may be a novel experience for many children.

There is nothing to stop you, if you have time – or can persuade a class-room assistant, parent or volunteer – making 'in house' recordings of other texts you want children to work on, so that they can listen and follow. Readily-available software tools now make it relatively easy to record such talking books and create mp3 files of them, or even burn them to CD.

> My husband – who had a few spare hours at the time – once read and recorded most of a short accessible novel for a Key Stage 3 pupil of mine who needed extra encouragement and support with her reading.

If older children in the school were involved in making the recordings, you would also be developing speaking, communication, drama and even ICT skills in these other students.

Use larger print

Research has shown that children can often read a book more easily if the print is larger. Sometimes a child will find a book too difficult, but is able to read an 'easy' version. The only difference, in some cases, is the size of the words printed on the page.

So if you've got a struggling reader, try offering a large print version (perhaps of a classic which they will have seen around the school, such as *The Wind in the Willows* or *The Silver Sword*) but let them think that it's a shorter, easier book. Then, when the book is finished, you can have the pleasure of boosting the child's self-esteem by explaining that the book was not 'easier' at all. The words were the same as in the 'full' version. So that child is now a fully-fledged reader!

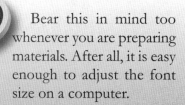

✐ That is why there are probably plenty of large print books – with content at all levels – in your school and its library. Many recent books for children have been published in more than one version, to accommodate large print needs.

Bear this in mind too whenever you are preparing materials. After all, it is easy enough to adjust the font size on a computer.

 ## Pay attention to fonts

✐ Publishers of books designed to be read by younger readers pay a lot of attention to the font used in the books. Children who are still learning to recognise individual letters need the letters to be presented in a clear and consistent way. The two biggest issues are usually with the letters 'a' and 'g': these should be written as 'ɑ' and 'g', and not in the more common form 'a' and 'g'.

✐ For older readers, publishers tend to be less concerned about the fonts used, as it is less of an issue for the more-able reader. However, struggling readers may still need the text to be presented in clear, simple fonts. Many specialist publishers of 'high-low' books will cater for older, struggling readers by choosing fonts with helpful letter forms.

Make sure that you always use fonts that can easily be read by the children you are working with.

Covert literacy activities

It's important to find ways of covertly developing the struggling reader's literacy skills, by subtly teaching 'literacy' at every opportunity – without making it too obvious that that's what you're doing.

Here are a few ways of doing that.

- Call it 'art' – but talk to the children about their drawing, painting, model-making etc. Encourage them to read and write captions for their work.

- If a child shows an interest in something, or asks a question, make a point of looking up the answer in a book or on the Internet – and then reading aloud what you have discovered (with your finger tracing the printed word).

- Read with the child. Look at an exciting or interesting book together. Let the child choose it. Read ten or so words aloud, pointing to the words as you go. Then stop at a simple word for the child to read. It might, to start with, just be one they can guess accurately. This is a very good way of building self-esteem unobtrusively.

 Be relaxed and keep a sense of humour. Don't ever let a child think that you are tense or frustrated about their lack of progress. It is counter-productive because the child will pick it up from you and become anxious too.

- Try not to 'show up' a weak reader by exposing them too often to the experience of hearing another child reading aloud effortlessly.

- Work on phonics at every opportunity – with games and activities.

It's OK – it's not literacy!

Have lots of books about. Make sure that the majority of books are illustrated – with engaging, age-appropriate illustrations. For children who can't or won't read, illustrations are the key to hooking them. Share the books and talk about them.

Build in as much small-group work as you can – informally as well as formally. It enables the adults in the classroom to give struggling readers more individual attention.

Try to get the parents on board – although they may have literacy difficulties themselves. Talk to them (if appropriate, in private, rather than in front of the child) about what they can do at home to complement what you are doing in school.

It's surprising how many parents simply don't understand how important it is to read to children.

Reading buddies

Some primary schools have a system of getting older children (children from Years 5 or 6 – ages 8 to 11 – and usually the struggling readers) to spend an hour or so a week 'helping' in Reception with small groups. Alternatively, sometimes an older child becomes a younger one's reading buddy or partner.

The advantages of such schemes are:

✎ Buddy-reading is a neat and tactful way of getting the older child to practise reading using the lower interest-age texts that would normally be rejected as 'baby stuff.'

✎ The older child finds that they can read enough to prompt the younger one. And they have to remind the younger child how to 'sound out' words too (phonics in action!). In other words, it helps to consolidate earlier learning in the older child.

✎ As every teacher knows, the very best way to learn – *really* learn – something is to explain or teach it to someone else.

It is a terrific confidence booster to a nine or 10 year old to be invited to be a temporary 'honorary' teacher – and if a child is still struggling with reading at that age they will have fragile self-confidence.

✎ The younger child has the fun of learning from or with someone who is a bit like an older brother or sister, and who may be less daunting than a grown-up. They can ask different sorts of questions.

✎ Establishing a good rapport between children in different year groups and making sure that they know each other militates against bullying in a school.

✎ It gives the younger child some individual or small-group attention that they might not otherwise get in a busy classroom staffed by a limited number of adults.

Paired reading schemes give reading a higher status in the school and encourage children to want to do it.

Some books are ideal for this kind of paired or 'buddy' reading.

The *Trailblazers* series, for example, published by Ransom Publishing, features fiction texts at two levels – a 'full text' version and a simpler 'speech bubble' comic-style version. These texts are on facing pages and give two entry points to the narrative.

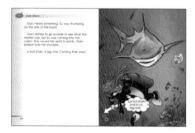 

Perfect for buddy reading: story spreads from the Trailblazers series, written by David and Helen Orme.

4 Meeting Individual Needs

4 Meeting Individual Needs

 # The Issues

 ## Every child is unique

Every child is unique. Every child has special – or individual – needs.

As we have already observed several times in this book, no two children (not even identical twins) are the same. Every child is different and that, of course, means that there are as many learning needs and learning styles as there are children.

Boys' needs are often different from girls'. And personality – along with the mysteries of brain chemistry and environmental factors such as the family we grow up in – all affect the way children learn.

> Some boys and girls learn to read quickly and easily. Others struggle.

The reasons why some children struggle are many and varied. For example:

 Just as children learn to sit up, speak and walk at different ages, so the timing of their arrival at reading readiness varies. It can be as simple as that.

Children who have had stories read to them before starting at school, who have been exposed to language and books and who have seen adults around them reading for pleasure, are more likely to take to reading themselves than those who live most of their lives in book-free or language-light environments. *Lily sees Mum read*

 Boys develop at a different pace and in a different way from girls. Many boys learn to read later than girls of the same age. Some researchers think that the difference can be as much as two years.

 Many twenty-first century children find it difficult to concentrate for long – possibly because of over-exposure to visual media such as TV, computer games and DVDs. Food additives may also be partly responsible.

 Toxic Childhood by Sue Palmer (Orion, 2006) has interesting things to say about the effects of twenty-first century life on children's development.

 ## Multiple intelligences

The American psychologist Howard Gardner (born 1943) believes that the view we generally hold on what constitutes intelligence and the ability to learn is far too narrow.

> Gardner has identified seven varieties of intelligence, which he calls 'multiple intelligences'.

Gardner's seven multiple intelligences are listed on the next page.

Few of us – and few of the children we work with, or are bringing up – are confined to just one of these, of course. Most of us have elements of several – and most of us lack one or more variety almost entirely.

It pays to try to understand your own mix of intelligences, as well as those of the children you work with.

Gardner's seven multiple intelligences

1. verbal – spatial

2. verbal – linguistic

3. logical – mathematical

4. bodily – kinesthetic

5. musical – rhythmical

6. interpersonal

7. intrapersonal

The child who is weak in verbal/linguistic intelligence – which their university-educated teachers are likely to be strong in – is often rather negatively seen as having 'learning difficulties'.

In fact it may just be a matter of harnessing the different sorts of intelligence which they *do* have and finding ways of applying them to reading. Be willing and ready to use numbers, logic, music or physical activity if that's where a child's strengths are.

For example, get a group of kinesthetically-inclined children to act out physically the phonic shape of a word. Each child could 'be' a letter or grapheme (with labels on their chests?).

Ask them to act out their sound – is it a hard consonant like /k/ – or is it a soft /oa/ for example? At the end, get the children to line up to form the word.

Or, if they have logical/mathematical strengths, they will probably enjoy code word games and crosswords – which are very useful activities for reading and spelling.

A musically and rhythmically intelligent child might be encouraged to sing or beat out the rhythms of words. You can make spelling aloud very sing-song and rhythmic if you wish. Poems and rhymes may be more useful than prose texts in this regard.

 # Learning styles

Gardner's seven intelligences can be refined into three main learning styles:

 ## Visual

Visual learners respond to body language and faces. They may think in pictures and take, or want to take, detailed notes.

 ## Auditory

Auditory learners respond to verbal lectures and oral instructions. They learn through discussion and they are more comfortable with, say, an audio-book than a print one.

 ## Tactile/kinesthetic

Kinesthetic learners need hands-on experience. They learn by moving, doing and touching. They are active 'explorers' and may find it difficult to sit still for long.

It is useful to bear this quite simple theory in mind when you are thinking about how you can meet the individual needs of the children whose reading you are trying to develop.

Boys

As Sue Palmer pointed out in a 2004 article for *Early Years Update*: '*Girls and boys come out to play*', boys, like their primate ancestors, have better developed right-brains than girls. (She has a lot more to say about this in her 2009 book *21ˢᵗ Century Boys*, published by Orion).

The male hormone, testosterone, accelerates right-brain growth. The right side of the brain deals with overviews, movement, creativity and visuo-spatial skills. The less developed left side is the organised bit responsible for language, logic, order and sequence.

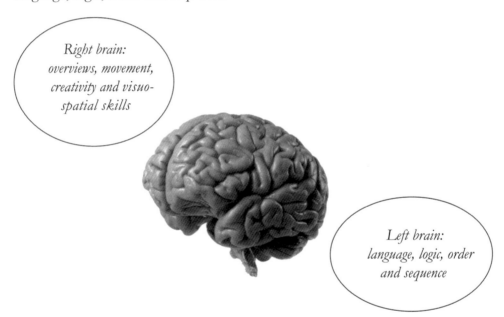

Right brain: overviews, movement, creativity and visuo-spatial skills

Left brain: language, logic, order and sequence

It dates back many millennia, of course, to a time when females, whose left brains were (and are) well developed, did not need the strong visuo-spatial ability and large-scale motor control required to take part in the hunt. They developed different strengths, relating to fine motor control and communication with the other females, as collaboration around the camp fire was important if their offspring were to survive.

> *'It's not,'* writes Sue Palmer, *'that they* (boys) *don't develop these left-brain skills eventually. It's just that they've got other important skills to develop as well. Skills that in the past, females didn't have much use for – although again, given suitable learning opportunities, females can also acquire all the right-brain skills. Male and female brains are potentially the same – and the most successful brains are the most balanced ones.'*

So in practice we have to be aware that boys are different. We have to look for ways of helping them to develop those left-brain skills which are so crucial to reading – without trying to force too much too soon.

Boys, of course, often have very specific interests. Football, fishing, other sports, computer games and dinosaurs are obvious examples, although there is a danger in stereotyping too much – because every child, as we've noted, is unique. I have worked with boys who are nuts about classical music, ferry boats, old buses and castles – to name but a few.

Whatever the specific interests are – and most children are interested in *something*, even if it's something as straightforward as a favourite TV programme – it's well worth harnessing these interests as a way of meeting individual needs, particularly in boys.

 Girls

Because most girls tend to be 'chattier' than most boys, there can be concentration problems when you are trying to persuade girls to apply their reading skills.

And, like boys, girls are more likely to read happily about things which interest them, rather than things imposed on them by an adult.

Look out for specific interests, too. If a girl is keen on tiger conservation, tennis or the newest, hottest pop band, then find some non-fiction reading material about it for her.

And girls really do like pink! Look around any bookshop and you will spot an enormous number of 'girly' novels with pink covers, totally off-putting to brothers, dads and male schoolteachers. But the publishers know what they're doing and these books have girl appeal — worth capitalising on if you're looking for books likely to grab their attention.

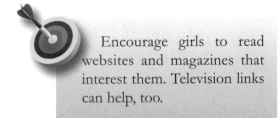

Encourage girls to read websites and magazines that interest them. Television links can help, too.

 ## Special Educational Needs

In a sense every child has 'special' needs because every child is, as we have already discussed, unique. However, we should distinguish between these kinds of special needs (which every child has) and *Special Educational Needs* (or SEN), which has a special meaning in educational circles.

> A child with SEN is a child who has a significantly greater difficulty in learning than the majority of pupils of their age, or has a disability which means that they cannot make full use of the general educational facilities provided for pupils of their age.

In practice, the term is most commonly taken to mean pupils who are, for whatever reason, behind their peers educationally and who have needs often labelled as a 'specific learning difficulty' (or SpLD). These include difficulties or disabilities such as dyslexia, dyspraxia, autism, Asperger Syndrome (or AS, and named after the twentieth century Austrian doctor who first described it) and attention-deficit hyperactivity disorder (ADHD).

However the term is also used to refer to children with moderate learning disabilities and physical disabilities (such as hearing, motor and visual disabilities).

Note that if a child has Special Educational Needs in literacy, they will probably be 'struggling', and therefore many (if not all) of the tips suggested in Chapter Three may be appropriate. However the converse is not necessarily true.

J ust because a child is struggling with reading does not mean that they have SEN.

In the UK, if teachers think that a child may have SEN, the child is referred for expert assessment. The result of this may be 'a statement of Special Educational Needs' and the child is often thereafter referred to as having been 'statemented'.

The statement officially sets out what the child's needs are and specifies the level of extra help they must receive. This could be, for example, part-time (or full-time) one-to-one help from a designated teaching assistant in the classroom. Or it could entitle the child to some small group work with a specialist teacher – among other possibilities.

Gifted and talented children – who often surge ahead with their reading and so need extra support, encouragement and guidance to develop it further – should certainly be regarded as having SEN.

R emember that almost every child can learn to read, if only we can find the right way of helping them.

Dyslexia

Dyslexia (the word, from Greek, means difficulty with words) is a life-long learning difficulty which affects the development of literacy and language-related skills. Dyslexics often have problems with phonological processing – or the ability to see/hear how phonemes fit together. And this disability is out of synch with the development of the individual's other cognitive skills. Some (but by no means all) dyslexics are talented musicians, actors or artists, for instance.

Many specific learning difficulties are invisible.

Dyslexia is, according to the British Dyslexia Association (*www.bdadyslexia.org.uk*), 'resistant to conventional teaching.' That means you have to find other effective ways of helping dyslexic children to learn.

Neil MacKay (*www.actiondyslexia.co.uk*) has argued for example that dyslexia should be thought of not as a disability but as a 'learning preference'.

This places the focus much more on the *process* implications of dyslexia, rather than on the consequence (problems with 'reading'). This view also shifts the onus to find an effective solution more towards the teacher, rather than just accepting that it is the learner's problem.

> *'Dyslexia as a learning preference means pupils have the right to be dyslexic and so have the right to receive, process and present information and concepts in preferred ways.'*
> Neil MacKay

✏️ With dyslexics, for example, make sure that all instructions are very clear and that all the work is structured step-by-step – exactly as most phonics programmes specify.

✏️ And experiment with coloured perspex. A lot of research has shown that dyslexics who find it very difficult to master reading skills sometimes find print much easier to decode if they view it through coloured film – and different people benefit from different colours. You could buy some perspex sheets and experiment.

Commercial products on the market include coloured screen overlays for computers, glasses with coloured lenses, bookmarks and other forms of flat, tinted transparent devices which the reader can pass over the print on a page.

 # Autistic Spectrum Disorder (ASD)

Autism is a life-long disability characterised by abnormal self absorption, to the extent that the individual doesn't respond to others and may have difficulty communicating. Some severely autistic children do not learn to speak.

Asperger Syndrome (AS) is a less extreme form of autism. The self-absorption is still there, along with the difficulty in relating to people. A child with AS may also have limited but obsessive interests.

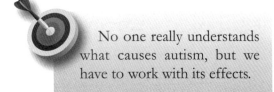

No one really understands what causes autism, but we have to work with its effects.

Specialists use the term 'autistic spectrum disorder' (or ASD) to describe the range of severity of the condition.

In practice, children at the more severe end of this spectrum are likely to be in special schools often run by charities such as the National Autistic

Society (*www.nas.org.uk*). But there are many statemented children with autistic tendencies or Asperger Syndrome in mainstream schools, as well as children with undiagnosed or mild autism or AS who are not (or not yet) statemented.

About half a million people in the UK are known to have an autistic spectrum disorder. That amounts to about one in 120 overall. And although children can wait up to three years for a diagnosis, more children than adults have been diagnosed, so it is certainly not uncommon in schools.

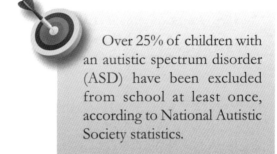

Over 25% of children with an autistic spectrum disorder (ASD) have been excluded from school at least once, according to National Autistic Society statistics.

In children, it is easy to mistake ASD for naughtiness or 'bad behaviour.'

Autism is probably one of the hardest conditions for an outsider to understand. If you are grappling with understanding what makes an autistic child tick, then read Mark Haddon's wonderful novel *The Curious Incident of the Dog in the Night-Time* – whose autistic hero is gifted and talented in Gardner's logical/mathematical intelligence.

I once visited a SEN school specifically for autistic pupils (run by the National Autistic Society) in which one class of 13 – 14 year olds (at Key Stage 3) was using Mark Haddon's novel as their class reader – an interesting idea.

Generally though, it's a question of working through the same activities as you would with any other child – in collaboration with the school's SEN coordinator and any other advice at your disposal. Give a child with an ASD as much individual attention as you can. Be patient and consistent – and that's where parents can do a wonderful job, too.

Given that many children with Asperger Syndrome have obsessive interests, it would make sense to focus reading materials and reading practice on these interests if you can – just as you would for any other child. Although since there are likely to be communication problems, it is even more important in this case to find a point of contact between you and the child.

Sometimes local specialist SEN schools offer training for colleagues in mainstream schools, especially with regard to autism. Make enquiries in your area.

Part Two

Creating Effortless Readers

5 Turning Them Into Readers

5 Turning Them Into Readers

The Issues

 ## Creating *real* readers

Far too many children learn the rudiments of reading at the ages of about 5 to 7 (Key Stage 1 in the UK) and more or less grasp it, but then fail to become long-term readers. Later they slip back. By the time, in England at least, they complete primary school and move on to secondary school (at the age of 10 or 11), some are effectively non-readers again.

This is partly because the children have not built up any reading stamina. This in turn is often because the teaching and encouragement stopped at the point when it should merely have changed gear and moved forward.

Nearly all children – at least those without severe disability – eventually learn to turn the squiggles on the page, paper, screen or notice board into words. However halting their reading is, very few children in the modern, developed world reach adulthood being totally unable to read.

Stumbling uncomprehendingly through a passage from a book, while an adult listens and corrects your mistakes, is not 'reading'. It's just decoding – or, as we said previously, barking at print.

Real reading is what you learn to do *after* you've cracked the basic code. That's when reading develops, grows and becomes part of you – or not.

It's all too easy for busy teachers to think that once Ryan, Jamila or Nicholas can 'read', you don't have to do any more because the job is done. You can tick the 'reading' box and hurry on to the next thing.

 Compare reading with driving a car. If you passed your driving test, walked out of the test centre and didn't get behind the wheel again for five or ten years, you would probably find that the skill had gone because you hadn't consolidated and developed it.

Reading is similar – except that, with reading, there isn't a point when you can say you have passed your test. Reading is a skill that needs to continue to be developed over a long period of time – certainly well into secondary school.

And what about the boy or girl who reads quite keenly at primary school, but loses interest in reading at secondary school when puberty sets in?

Boys in particular need careful managing because, for whatever reason, they are less likely to take to fiction than girls. Therefore teachers have to find other ways of keeping boys hooked.

It's not just a 'school' problem, either. Many parents who do read with their children whilst they are learning to read, abandon the habit once their children are able to read on their own.

Subvocalising

When a child first learns to read, they read every word aloud. Then they progress to reading every word aloud to themselves – 'inside their head' but without speaking.

However, although the children may seem to be reading to themselves, or reading silently, in fact they are not yet reading in the same way as experienced readers. Children who have just begun to read 'inside their heads' are, in fact, doing exactly the same as if they were reading aloud – except that they are not actually speaking. Their jaw muscles, for example, often move as they read, mimicing the sound that they would make if they were reading aloud.

This is a technique called subvocalising.

> Fast, fluent readers don't subvocalise when they are reading normally. A fluent reader can read quickly for meaning without having to translate each individual word into a sound or set of sounds.

For fluent readers, the brain learns to convert signs seen by the eye into meaning without consciously passing through the medium of spoken or heard words. This is how most of us read, and it is what we should aim for in the children we work with.

Some children don't make the jump to fluent reading. They get stuck at the early 'inside their head' phase and go on subvocalising for the rest of their lives.

Subvocalisers read very slowly. Many of them, as a result, find reading boring. It takes them a long time to extract meaning because the process is so laborious. Often they turn to other sources (such as television) for entertainment, and spend ever less time reading or trying to read.

It is therefore essential that we find ways of moving the subvocalisers on.

> All pupils, for example, need sacred blocks of time every day when they read independently and silently. As with any other skill, the more you do it the faster you get.

And it's partly a matter of acquiring the confidence to stop using subvocalising as a prop – a bit like leaving the edge of the swimming pool and striking out for the middle.

Getting books into young hands

Libraries are key to getting children reading. Most schools have a library, large or small. The smallest primary school libraries are usually teacher-managed. Some big secondary schools have a qualified librarian on the staff. In many schools there will also be book corners or class libraries for younger classes.

In secondary schools, many English departments make use of book boxes, which can work well too. These are collections of books, offering a wide range of reading levels in both fiction and non-fiction, sometimes based around a theme. Book boxes are usually either a resource purchased by the English department, or they are loaned to the department and changed regularly by the school library. Students then borrow from the book boxes for independent reading.

Some schools also run bookshops or clubs, through which books are sold to pupils (often at a discounted price or with the profits going to the school fund) as another way of raising the profile of reading.

Some independent book-shops are willing to provide stock on a sale or return basis.

The Literacy Trust (*www.literacytrust.org.uk*) has a useful list on its website of specialist children's book-shops in the UK.

The purpose of all of this – obviously – is to make as many books as possible available to the pupils, in order to encourage wider, faster, more committed reading.

 ## Public Libraries

It's important to introduce pupils – of any age – to public libraries, as part of routine curriculum work. Many children come from families for whom library use and books are not part of life. So they do not know what is inside the library and what it can offer.

Most library staff will organise an introductory session for school groups and show them round the library. Many public libraries run after-school and holiday events for children. Particularly at primary level, if you can get the

Many children and young adults are not aware of what their local public library can offer.

children excited about the library, they may work on their parents to take them there again. Visiting the library is something that can easily be turned into a habit, part of the weekly routine.

 As a teacher, you could liaise with the local library to support topics being studied at school.

So, for example, if children are studying the Egyptians at school, try to arrange a display (or even better, Egyptian-related activities, such as making a mummy or Egyptian writing) at the local library. This helps tie children into the habit of going to their library.

One school I know set two pieces of homework as alternatives: the easier option could be done at the local library as part of a library-organised activity; the harder alternative had to be done at home. Needless to say, the library was very busy that week.

Hooking your pupils up with the public library is yet another way of getting them to regard reading as part of life. It maximises their exposure to books and introduces them to other adults who regard books as really important.

But, and it's a big 'but', it is an old truism that you can lead a horse to water but you cannot make it drink. Some children are already 'turned off' reading

> Arrange with the library staff for your class to visit the local public library. Then pupils can meet the children's librarian (and other staff), they can see the facilities and discover that there are many more books there than at school.

– perhaps because of the dull way it has been presented to them – before they have a chance to become real readers. Television and other media offering 'fast food' stories and entertainment are more attractive.

So, whether you are a teacher or a parent, look for books which link to TV programmes and films that the child is already interested in. Don't be afraid to encourage them to read comics.

Or, if *Pride and Prejudice* just isn't attractive enough for boy readers, why not *Pride and Prejudice and Zombies* by Seth Grahame-Smith? (Jane Austen is credited as co-author.) It largely follows the original text, but is set in a parallel universe full of … zombies. It may not win a literary award, but has plenty of 'boy-cool' factor.

Anything which gets them to engage with print helps to embed the reading habit.

5 Turning Them Into Readers

Practical Teaching Ideas

Providing adult role-models

Children learn by imitating adults.

If children see adults absorbed in (and enjoying) books, they come to regard reading as a normal part of grown-up life. If, on the other hand, adults in positions of influence – such as teachers – say they are too busy to read because they have other, more important things to do, then children are likely to stop reading at the earliest opportunity because not reading 'feels' like grown-up behaviour.

It is therefore essential for young people to see lots of adult 'role-models' reading books.

> As children hit puberty, their interests change and the 'reading habit' they have (hopefully) acquired comes under increased pressure. This is when adult role-models can be particularly important in helping to protect and 'shore up' the child's reading habit.

What teachers can do

If you are a teacher, here are the top tips to promote reading amongst the children you work with.

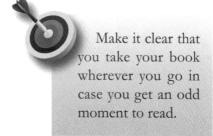

- Always have a book with you that you are in the process of reading. Make sure that everybody can see it sticking out of your bag or on the corner of your desk. Show that books are important to you.

  Make it clear that you take your book wherever you go in case you get an odd moment to read.

- Let the children see you reading for pleasure.

 Talk about the books you are reading. Talk about the characters, or the situations that they find themselves in. Discuss some of the plot issues with the children.

Show that reading is rewarding.

- Talk to parents about the importance of providing reading role-models at home. Make practical suggestions about how they can help their children with reading.

  It can need handling with tact but, for example, boys who see dads and other men in their lives reading are probably more likely to become readers than those who don't.

✏ If the class or group is reading silently, then you read too. If you undertake any other activity, you are suggesting that that is more important than reading. It isn't (except in the direst of emergencies, such as to tend a sick child).

✏ Talk informally with the children about books and about reading. Do it often.

✏ Present yourself as someone who never leaves home bookless, who sometimes forgets to wash up because you're so deep in your book, who often can't remember whether you've read the book or seen the film ... and so on. Tell them the things you never leave home without (house keys, money, mobile phone, book ...).

> The children may laugh at, and with, you – but they will register the fact that books can be fantastially rewarding, and some will copy you.

B ecome a book fanatic. Make it clear how much pleasure reading books gives you.

✏ Tell them about books you enjoyed when you were their age – and/or about books your own children have liked.

✏ Listen to what children tell you about books they have read which you haven't. Make a point of reading some of them and then feeding back your thoughts.

It is very gratifying for a child if a teacher heeds a recommendation and spends time exploring it. It gives real status to reading.

Adults – especially dads – can be powerful role-models.

 ## What parents can do

And here are the top tips for parents.

 Make a point of reading any book, or comic, or whatever else your child reads, so that you can discuss it with them.

 If the book relates to a TV programme or film, chat about which was better and why.

> What can a book do that a film can't? What can a film do which a book can't?
>
> Why, for example, is the plot of the film version of a book nearly always simpler than the original book?

Read as much as you can yourself – books, magazines, newspapers, websites – whatever. Make sure you let your children see you doing it. This applies particularly to dads and sons, so that boys grow up thinking that reading is an OK, 'blokish' thing to do.

 Go to the library or bookshop (or look at on-line bookshops) with your child so that you choose books and/or magazines together – and they see that you are interested in reading.

Getting help from heroes

It really encourages young readers if they discover that their heroes and heroines (film stars, premier league footballers, pop musicians, etc.) value reading too.

Famous sports personalities are great role-models to promote reading.

Several of the big football clubs in Britain run literacy education programmes, whereby players go into schools to encourage reading. This is usually done alongside coaching the children in football and inviting them to the ground as an incentive.

> If you are a teacher it is worth contacting your local club to see what's on offer, if anything. Or take the initiative and start a partnership with the club.

 At a national level, the UK Government's *Playing for Success* scheme works to motivate pupils through study support centres at sports clubs. During the National Year of Reading (2008) many Premier League and First Division Clubs joined in the scheme, and others joined in local partnerships with, for example, libraries or Local Authorities, to promote reading. This work continues.

 The UK's National Literacy Trust also runs *Reading the Game*, an initiative to promote literacy through sport. Many Premier League football clubs (for example) have players directly involved in this scheme. You can find out more at *www.literacytrust.org.uk/reading_the_game.html*.

 ## Listening and following

Make use of audio-books. These are available on CD from high street and on-line book-shops, and also as downloads from websites such as Amazon, Audible.com or via iTunes.

In a busy classroom, or in the living room or kitchen at home, you can easily set children up with headphones so that others are not disturbed.

✏ Encourage a child listening to an audio-book to follow the story in the book as it is read to them. Doing so binds reading and listening together.

Many audio-books contain abridged versions of the text. If the child is listening to an abridged audio-book, it may not be easy to follow with the printed book.

✏ For a child learning to read, there are advantages to listening to a recording whilst following the written text. For example:

✓ It develops listening skills.

✓ It helps to build concentration span.

✓ It boosts confidence, because the child feels as if they are actually reading.

✓ Even if the child listens and follows without much adult support, they will still acquire some whole-word recognition.

✓ If a grown-up is available to work on the phonics opportunities afterwards, it puts valuable learning into an enjoyable context.

✓ In time, if a child has listened and followed the same text several times, they will begin to know it by heart.

 When you hear a child 'reading' the book aloud without the audio-book, you know that they are really progressing.

Getting authors into school

Many children's authors visit schools to talk to the children about the books they've written and to encourage them to read. Many will spend a whole day in a school working with different groups. David and Helen Orme, for example, who have written many, many books for children, make a large number of school visits every year.

> **Y**oung people love meeting the individuals behind the names on the covers of books, and it is a powerful way of encouraging reading.

Children often want to read some of the books before they meet a writer, or, if not, they are often motivated and curious to read the books after meeting them. Most authors bring copies of their books with them, so that pupils – advised in advance to bring some money – can buy them and get them signed. (You could always invite parents along too, and let them do the buying.) Authors will usually happily sign copies of their books already owned by children or by the school.

 You can approach writers by first contacting the publishers of their books (publisher contact details are printed at the front of all books). The National Association of Writers in Education (*www.nawe.co.uk*) has a directory on its website of authors who make school visits. The Society of Authors may also be able to help (*www.society ofauthors.org*). Another useful website is *www.ContactAnAuthor.co.uk*. In the USA *http://usawrites4kids.drury.edu/* is a good source of information and advice.

In addition, many authors now have their own website, so a quick Internet search might get you directly in touch with the author.

The Literacy Trust has helpful advice about authors in UK schools, on its website at *www.literacytrust.org.uk*.

As self-employed people, authors visiting schools do, of course, have to charge for their time, so if this isn't part of your school budget you will have to find a way of paying for it. The school's Parent Teacher Association (PTA) might help for instance, or there might be a local business which would sponsor it.

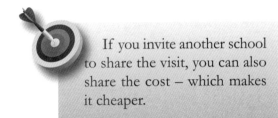

If you invite another school to share the visit, you can also share the cost – which makes it cheaper.

 ## Book reviews

Tell children that they don't have to take your word for it that a particular book is worth reading.

> **B**ook reviews can help to interest children in stories and novels.

So try to have plenty of reviews available.

 All newspapers and many magazines – including specialist ones such as The School Librarian, Books for Keeps (*www.booksfor keeps.co.uk*) and Carousel – carry reviews of books for children and young people. There are many websites too, offering good, impartial book reviews, such as (in the UK) The Guardian news-paper's *Building a children's library* (*www.guardian.co.uk/books/building achildrenslibrary*).

> If you can obtain reviews written, not by adults but by other children, so much the better.
> Children are much more likely to accept recommendations from their peers than from adults (especially from teachers).

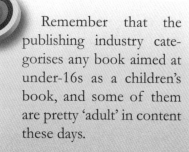

 The Literacy Trust (*www.literacy trust.org.uk*) has a list of websites which review children's books. And there are, of course, hundreds of reviews on websites – some written by professionals and others by ordinary readers.

Remember that the publishing industry categorises any book aimed at under-16s as a children's book, and some of them are pretty 'adult' in content these days.

 You can often trigger an interest in a book by reading (or showing) young readers a review of it. Depending on the age of the children, you might then pin the review on a notice board and/or put a link to it on the school's Intranet – not forgetting to ensure that there are copies of the book available in the classroom or school library so that any interested child can get it easily.

 Children also learn by writing their own book reviews (or by giving oral presentations on the books). In this way they can recommend books to each other.

It is best not to be judgmental about their choices though. Within reason, let them share the books they really enjoyed. The idea is to get them reading freely and eclectically.

Later, once they have become compulsive readers, you can drip-feed awareness of 'better' or more challenging books if you need to.

 Publish the children's reviews in the school magazine or on a class webpage, or build them into an assembly.

Give the children's reviews as much status as you can, to show that you take their reading and their views very seriously.

If you are a parent, encourage your child regularly to write reviews of books they read and post them on the Internet. There is a facility to do this at *www.amazon.co.uk*, for example.

Using shared readers

If you are a teacher, sometimes you and a group or class will be reading a novel as a 'class reader'. How are you going to manage the reading, learning and shared experience?

> The problem with shared reading of a full-length novel is that it tends to take a long time – several weeks if you read, say, a chapter a day.

So there are two challenges: how to structure the reading, and how to keep everyone interested.

Structuring shared reading

 You need to decide how to do the reading.

? Will you read aloud to the class while they follow you with the text?

? Or will you get class members to take it in turns to read aloud?

? Or will they read some chapters in companionable silence and then read a section aloud when everyone has got to it?

? Will you ask them to read the occasional chapter for home-work?

? Or do you favour a combination of all these – or some other method?

The answer, of course, depends on the size, age and reading ability of the group.

And there are always some children who, as faster readers, will be frustrated, whilst other, slower readers may be left behind – because we all read at different speeds.

 ## Keeping everyone interested

You need to keep everyone interested while the novel-sharing proceeds.

The aim is always to encourage the children to think more carefully about their reading.

Fortunately there are plenty of activities which can work well in this regard. The following ideas can be adapted to work at any level.

- Children work in pairs to guess and talk about how the novel might end.

- One child pretends to be one of the characters from the novel. They talk to the group about their thoughts, character, actions, family, etc. Other children have to guess which character the child is.

- Write a letter from one character to another.

- Make a frieze of characters for the classroom wall. Make each child responsible for a drawing, painting, etc. and for cutting out a character.

- Make up, or write, a story with the same setting.

> For example, write a riverbank story if you're reading *The Wind in the Willows*, or a seventeenth century story if you're on Sally Gardner's *I, Coriander*.

Make a timeline showing events in the novel. Build it up on the classroom wall as you go along.

 If (as in *Wuthering Heights*, *Rebecca* or Michael Morpurgo's *Billy the Kid*) there are time shifts and flashbacks, this can really help with the understanding of the plot.

Whatever the shared novel is, don't forget to have copies of similar books, and others by the same author, available for the children to move on to independently.

 Parents can share books with their children at home, too.

If you read to the child at bedtime, you and they can take it turns to read – if the child's reading is up to it.

You can also chat at other times about where you think the book is going, what will happen next, which character you each like best, and so on.

Making use of films

Many children's books have been filmed for the cinema or television and are now available on DVD (or for download).

For example the following movies are all now available on DVD: *The Chronicles of Narnia, The Railway Children, One Hundred and One Dalmatians, Mary Poppins, The Worst Witch, Watership Down, Charlotte's Web*, the *Harry Potter* series, *The Lord of the Rings* – as well as many others.

Sometimes it helps to show one of these films to a group of children as a way of getting interest. Then you can introduce them to the book.

Many books for teenagers and young adults have also been made into films. Philip Pullman's *His Dark Materials* trilogy has spawned the film *The Golden Compass*, and there are plenty of 'classics' about – such as filmed versions of the Dickens or Brontë novels.

A child who might struggle with a particular book 'cold' will often cope with it more easily once they have seen a dramatisation.

On the other hand, it also makes sense sometimes (e.g. with slightly more able readers) to tell them that you will let them see the film as a treat, once the group has finished reading the book.

Some children may be disappointed with the film (which might have cut bits out and represented the characters differently from how the reader imagined).

In which case you've made an important point: that reading offers different rewards.

For example, with junior groups watch the 2005 film of *Charlie and the Chocolate Factory*, starring Johnny Depp.

Many children may have read the book, but some probably won't have done so.

 Get them to choose their favourite passages from the book and present them to the group.

Lead them on to explore some of Roald Dahl's other children's titles, such as *James and the Giant Peach*, *The Twits* and *Charlie and the Great Glass Elevator*.

Children who have read these can give oral reviews for the rest of the class.

Or, for groups aged over 11, try one of the many filmed versions of *Pride and Prejudice*.

The 2005 film directed by Joe Wright and starring Keira Knightley is pretty authentic and very watchable.

Then read aloud some of the novel's key passages, such as the famous opening, or the section in which Darcy finally proposes and is accepted. Or one of the funny passages in which Mrs Bennet is being outrageous, or Mr Collins obnoxious.

If you enthuse enough, some children will be encouraged to tackle the book independently – and then there are five other glorious Jane Austen novels to explore.

The public library is good place to borrow films, if there's no money in the school budget to buy them.

Or, in the UK, try the DVD rental service Love Film (*www.lovefilm.com*).

USSR (or ERIC)

We have mentioned independent reading and its importance before, but I make no apology for revisiting it, because once a child has learned to decode text, it is probably the most important of all classroom activities.

Known in the past by quirky names such as USSR (Uninterrupted Sustained Silent Reading) or ERIC (Everyone Reads in Class), time for pupils to read independently (while the teacher and classroom/teaching/ learning assistants read too, to show that it really matters) has been slowly eroded over the years, as the curriculum has become more crowded.

ERIC: Everyone Reads In Class. **USSR**: Uninterrupted Sustained Silent Reading. **NMMR**: Nothing Matters More than Reading.

> Too many teachers nowadays are pressurised into seeing independent reading as a cop-out – perhaps because it is something that they and the children might really enjoy together.

Silent reading in class

So if you need to justify silent reading in class (and I hope you don't) here are some good reasons why it matters so much.

✍ Because reading is private and individual, it allows choice – which the children rarely get in school.

- It is a fine form of differentiated learning because, perhaps with a bit of guidance, each individual can choose what they are capable of reading.

- It gives the teacher a chance to model good practice by reading for twenty minutes or more.

- It creates a peg for the teacher to discuss reading with individual students.

- It is a good opportunity for formative assessment of children.

And NEVER forget that ERIC or USSR is a time when 'we read' not when 'you read'.

Set the children to read while you do something else – such as marking – at your peril, because it 'says' that reading is a childish thing which you have outgrown now that you have important, adult responsibilities.

NMMR
(**N**othing **M**atters **M**ore than **R**eading).

Make it your mantra and put it on the classroom wall.

6 Reading Poems, Songs and Verses

6 Reading Poems, Songs and Verses

 The Issues

Don't ignore poetry

Don't ignore poetry. Or worse, don't patronise your charges by assuming that poetry is too difficult or too 'literary' for them.

The fact is that children – even the struggling and/or truculent ones – often enjoy it. Poetry is usually short. It's often fun, and there's something intangibly satisfying about the way words lock together poetically (back to *West Bromwich Albion* and so on), especially if there's plenty of rhyme and alliteration.

> Poetry is another handy piece of kit in the armoury of the teacher aiming to develop reading, or the parent trying to encourage it.

 Bear in mind, though, that poetry is closely related to music (the ancient Greeks had only one word for both) and often benefits from being *heard*, rather than being read silently.

And that applies particularly to rap, which boys (especially) tend to love. Then there's reggae and Caribbean music: song and poetry waiting to be tapped. For older children for example, you could use the work of artists such as Linton Kwesi Johnson and Benjamin Zephaniah. Or 'punk poet' John Cooper Clark and Attila the Stockbroker, too.

Cast the net as wide as you can.

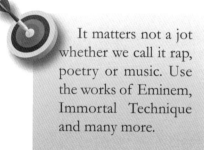

It matters not a jot whether we call it rap, poetry or music. Use the works of Eminem, Immortal Technique and many more.

 ## Poetry and prose

Poems can sometimes – rather usefully – point older students back to prose fiction, because so many writers have been inspired by the work of poets.

 For example, *Alone on a Wide Wide Sea* by Michael Morpurgo relates to Coleridge's famous poem *The Ancient Mariner*.

You could first introduce the students to the poem (or to extracts from it) that inspired the novel. Use the poem as a springboard for the novel. Read a chapter of the novel aloud and then have copies for interested students to take away and continue reading.

Or introduce them first to the novel. Then share part (or all) of the poem that inspired it.

 ## Nursery rhymes

For the very youngest children, there are some good 'spin-off' stories based on nursery rhymes – the first poetry most of us learn.

For example:

> *Clever Polly and the Stupid Wolf* by Catherine Storr.
> *Each Peach Pear Plum* by Janet and Allan Ahlberg.
> *The Jolly Postman: Or Other People's Letters* by Janet and
> Allan Ahlberg.

 ## Narrative poetry

Most children and young people enjoy poems which tell stories.

> There are some very old and famous narrative poems, such as the ballad *Sir Patrick Spens*, along with poems by Wordsworth, Tennyson and many more.
>
> There are also more modern story poems. Try poets like Charles Causley, Wendy Cope, Grace Nichols and Kit Wright.

 ## Funny poems

Younger children often like funny poems. Try Thomas Hood's *November*, Ogden Nash's poems or Edward Lear's limericks. There's also Benjamin Zephaniah's verses in Afro-Caribbean dialect, or the poems of John Agard. All of these might be new to them.

Pam Ayres, Roger McGough, Michael Rosen and Roald Dahl have, amongst many others, written a lot of poetry which often manages to be thoughtful as well as funny.

Some poetry suggestions

The following poems are all old favourites with perennial appeal.

For ages 8 – 12 try:

Night Mail by W. H. Auden
The Pied Piper of Hamelin
    by Robert Browning
Jabberwocky by Lewis Carroll
Matilda by Hilaire Belloc
The Highwayman by Alfred Noyes.

Over 12s might like:

Cowboy Song by Charles Causley
The Eve of St Agnes by John Keats
Snake by D. H. Lawrence
The Lady of Shalot by Alfred Tennyson
The Ruined Maid by Thomas Hardy
The Journey of the Magi by T. S. Eliot.

And here are some less familiar poems that you might like to try with your children.

For ages 8 – 12 try:

Sally by Phoebe Hesketh
The Hills by Rachel Field
Is the Moon Tired? by Christina Rossetti
Our Solar System by Eric Finney
The Animals' Arrival
    by Elizabeth Jennings.

Worth looking at with over 12s:

The Young Wife by Derek Walcott
Tianamen by James Fenton
Like a Flame by Grace Nichols
In the Desert Knowing Nothing
    by Helen Dunmore
The Soldier by Rupert Brooke
Who's Who by Benjamin Zephaniah.

 ## Sources of poetry

John Foster – a really imaginative and very prolific anthologist – has compiled these anthologies (among many others), all published by Oxford University Press:

Monster Poems
Dragon Poems
Pet Poems
Dinosaur Poems
Fantastic Football Poems
Ghost Poems
Completely Crazy Poems
Fiendishly Funny Poems.

Other useful sources of poems include:

One Hundred Years of Poetry for Children
Young Dragon Book of Verse
    both ed. Michael Harrison & Christopher Stuart-
    Clark
Talking Turkeys by Benjamin Zephaniah.

If you are looking for a specific poet or poem, try googling the name of the poem or poet. But be copyright aware (see page 148, below).

There is a good selection of well-known poetry at *www.poetry-online.org*, which you and/or your pupils can download free.

Football (again)

If that *Fantastic Football Poems* anthology mentioned above caught your eye then, whether you are a parent or a teacher, look too at *www.footballpoets.org* which has some upbeat poems about the 'beautiful game.'

There is new work by young unknowns being posted on the site every day – all likely to appeal to youngsters, especially boys.

6 Reading Poems, Songs and Verses

Practical Teaching Ideas

Creating opportunities for poetry

✐ Whenever there's a very short time slot, suggest that children read poems to themselves or (better!) to each other in pairs.

✐ In school, try reading any sort of verse aloud when there's a tiny space to fill, such as two minutes at the end of a lesson. Then tell your children where and how to find more poems like that one – same poet, same subject, same rhythm or whatever. Remember that there's a lot of poetry on the Internet, if that's preferable to a big, daunting anthology.

✐ Keep anthologies handy in the classroom and use a computer to create some home-made wall posters of poems, song lyrics, raps or whatever. Or buy some ready-made ones.

✐ You can buy CDs of poetry, too. Some children might like to listen (on headphones) to poems and follow the poem in a book

There's never a bad time (or place) to read poetry.

at the same time. Listening and following, as we saw in Chapter Three, can help to build confidence.

✐ You can also use an electronic whiteboard to display a poem. If you're not using the whiteboard for something else, you could have the poem displayed on it like a wall display. Some children will certainly read it if it's there.

Why not use a poem for your screen saver?

✐ Have a session in the week when everyone reads poetry – not with you 'teaching' it (or labouring it?), but just for pleasure – and that all-important reading development. And don't forget, you are a role-model. Let them see you gobbling it up with relish, too.

Ten things to do with a poem

1. Write it out and give it to someone as a gift.

2. Search for other poems like it – on the same subject or by the same poet.

3. Learn it by heart.

4. Turn it into an improvised (or rehearsed) play.

5. Use it as a starting point for children's own writing (either poetry or prose).

6. Devise a set of questions about it and give them to another child to answer.

7. Set it to music.

8. Paint, draw or sculpt something inspired by it.

9. Share it with the rest of the school in an assembly.

10. Read it aloud in pairs, using different voices and accents.

Why not photocopy this list and put it on the wall in your classroom?

And for goodness' sake don't worry if they don't know the meaning of every word.

 Never be 'heavy' about poetry reading. That's the attitude which has traditionally put children off it.

> T. S. Eliot (who wrote all those lovely cat poems about Macavity, Gus, Bustopher Jones and so on – which the musical *Cats* is based on, as well as some serious stuff) said that poetry can communicate before it is understood – and he was right.

 Parents, too, could read a couple of poems with children at bedtime, as an alternative to a story.

 ## Personal poetry anthologies

Many youngsters enjoy creating their own poetry anthologies. Anyone who finds a poem they really like can feel the urge to 'own' it in some way.

 Traditionally, creating a personal anthology meant to copy the poem into a special notebook or on a sheet to put in a folder. And that, of course, is still fine. If it appeals, do it.

 Making electronic copies is another possibility. Poems can be typed and then printed creatively in a wide range of fonts and colours, for inclusion in a ring binder. Or a digital anthology could be created on the computer.

Teachers (or parents) could do this too. Then the adult can share their anthology with the children and role-model a real love of poetry reading, which some children will then want to emulate.

The lives of poets

Many poets live – or lived – rather dramatic lives.

If a reader likes a particular poem, you can sometimes interest them in reading about the life of the poet – in the same way that they are usually quite keen to read about the private life of a soap star, pop singer or footballer.

On the page opposite is just a tiny selection of poets whose stories might interest pupils.

 There is plenty of information about poets' lives in biographies, companions to English Literature, encyclopaedias and on the Internet.

Poets in school

Many poets see school visits as part of their work, and you can sometimes get external funding to help pay for it. The poets themselves can usually tell you if there are likely to be grants available, and how to apply for them.

If not – as with novelists and other writers – try local sponsors or the Parent-Teachers' Association. Also try to persuade the school bursar or business manager to factor some author visits (of all genres) into the school's budget.

 Like novelists, poets can be contacted via their publishers. Some have individual websites with contact details.

The interesting lives of poets

- **Elizabeth Barrett Browning**, who eloped aged 40 (and bore a child), having always been an invalid.

- **U. A. Fanthorpe**, winner of the Queen's Gold Medal for Poetry, who died in 2009 after a long relationship with another female writer, whom she met when they were both teachers in the same school.

- **Percy Bysshe Shelley** who, already married, eloped with a girl of 17, and drowned at the age of 30.

- **Ted Hughes** whose wife, another poet **Sylvia Plath**, committed suicide.

- **Frieda Hughes**, daughter of Ted Hughes and Sylvia Plath, also a poet.

- **Grace Nichols** and **John Agard** – two black poets married to each other.

- **John Clare**, who had serious mental health problems.

- **John Keats**, who died of a lung disease aged only 26.

- **Christina Rossetti**, who wrote passionate religious poetry and was the sister of a famous painter.

- **Walter Raleigh**, who was executed.

- **Samuel Taylor Coleridge**, who was a drug addict.

- **Charles Causley**, who died in 2003 having lived most of his life in his native Cornwall, except for Navy service in World War 2 (which features in his early poems).

Poets who engage well with young people include Grace Nichols, Wendy Cope and Kit Wright.

 ## Preparation

The secret to a successful school visit lies in very careful preparation.

You can prepare for a poet's visit in the following ways:

- Read with the children as many of the poet's poems as possible, and encourage the children to read their poems independently.

- Encourage the children to read as widely as possible about the poet's life, background and achievements. The Internet is probably the best source of information for this.

 ## A note on copyright

When you are making copies of other people's writing, you have to be mindful of the law. Teach children about copyright law, too.

In Britain, if a poet or author has been dead for 70 years or more, the copyright on his or her work has expired. So there is no problem.

If it's more recent – a work by someone alive or who has died within the last 70 years – there is no law against making a handwritten copy for your own use. But you must not sell it or publish it without permission. That is a form of theft and is punishable by law.

Almost all countries have copyright laws, and teachers and parents should check out the details before they make copies of poems (and other written material).

- Ask the poet for a CV in advance, and make sure that the children have read it, or that you have looked at it with them, before the visit.

- Sell some of the poet's books in school beforehand. (You can probably get them from the publisher or from a bookshop on sale or return.)

 With books in hand, the children are even more likely to read the poems.

Then, when the poet comes, they can be asked to sign the children's copies.

- Make arrangements for the children to be able to buy poetry books (which the poet will almost certainly have with them for sale).

- Invite parents, other staff, pupils from other schools, local librarians and so on to the session. It helps to keep the cost down if you spread it, and it raises the status and profile of the visit.

 # Alphabet rap

And one last thought. If you want a very basic literacy activity, ask the children to find a way of reciting the alphabet as a rap.

- Try getting the children to make up their own rhyme or song to help them learn it.

- You could even get them to make up a mnemonic alphabet activity for younger children, and then create an opportunity for them to try it out.

7 Reading for Information

7 Reading for Information

 The Issues

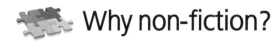 Why non-fiction?

Some children just don't take to fiction, and since most teachers present fiction as the main way into reading, this can be the very thing that puts some children off.

 Take my own father, for example. Although he was a very competent early reader, he was bored silly by fiction. He avidly read biographies, newspapers, manuals, history, reference books and a lot more besides.

But he couldn't see any point in reading things which 'weren't true'. In fact he swore in adulthood and in old age that he hadn't read a novel since an English teacher forced him through *Stalky and Co.* (by Rudyard Kipling) when he was at secondary school in the early 1930s.

Such people are a minority, but there are children like my father in every class, especially among boys.

So we need to find other ways to help into reading those who don't like fiction.

There is in fact a wide range of text-based information sources that can be used by children – some of which you may not have thought of using. These include reference books (obviously), newspapers and magazines, the Internet, and non-fiction books of various kinds.

Let's look at each in turn.

A lot of the information we look for can be found on the Internet these days, and we shall turn to that shortly. But encyclopaedias, dictionaries and other reference books are still very useful as a way of developing reading.

 ## Reference books

Sometimes it can actually be quicker to turn to a book close by, than to work laboriously through (for example) an Internet search engine.

Reference books may not be so fashionable these days, but they can be powerful motivators when it comes to reading.

If I want, say, the dates of a king, I always turn to my one-volume *Hutchinson Encyclopaedia*. If I want to look up a spelling or meaning, I use the *Collins English Dictionary*, which sits within inches of my keyboard.

Newspapers

Similarly, don't underestimate newspapers. They are an invaluable source of information about politics, international events, science, discoveries, sport, the arts, health, and (especially at weekends) many other topics. In an ideal world, newspapers would be part of every youngster's daily reading.

In the UK, there is a long tradition of newspaper reading and more newspapers are published here than in most other countries.

It is a missed opportunity if young people don't acquire the habit of reading newspapers.

Unfortunately, fewer than 50% of UK households ever buy a newspaper and the figure is even lower in many other countries. As our news reading habits migrate on-line, this figure is likely to decline. However, whilst newspapers are still with us, we should make use of them.

Magazines

There is at least one specialist magazine for just about every leisure interest you can think of — and many more for interests that you didn't know existed. Browse through the magazine listings in *Writers' and Artists' Yearbook* or *Writer's Handbook* (both in the reference section of most public libraries) for a sense of the range. Or take half an hour to look at the range available in a large newsagents.

Sometimes reluctant readers – especially boys – can be persuaded to read quite substantial articles in magazines devoted to subjects which really interest them.

Football titles are an obvious example, along with anything relating to other sports.

When I was a young teacher in charge of a school library in a 'tough' boys' school in London, I found I could coax dozens of boys – who wouldn't have dreamed of picking up a book – through my doors to read *The Angling Times*.

Non-readers they certainly weren't. They soaked up complex articles about fishing like blotting paper. It was a real boost to literacy and the status of reading in that school.

Many pupils are interested in technology, films, celebrities, pop culture, various sorts of crafts, and the environment. Many popular television programmes (such as *Top Gear*) also have magazines available to complement the programmes.

The Internet

When the Internet first really emerged in the early 1990s (strange to reflect just how young it still is) people said that it would kill reading.

In fact, the opposite has happened.

> Because nearly everything on the Internet has to be read – using all the traditional reading skills – it actually helps to develop reading.

It just means that most of us now turn to the Internet for the sort of practical information – railway timetables, phone numbers or street maps, for example – which we would once have got from print directories or books.

Using the Internet – especially web-based resources – *is* reading. Since children spend so much time there, we need actively to harness this to improve literacy.

A note on reading on-screen

Glare from the computer monitor, combined with a poor resolution (i.e. quality) compared to the printed page, makes reading on-screen more demanding and hence more tiring. (The printed page offers a minimum of 300 dots per inch, or dpi; books are usually printed at 600 dpi or higher. Yet the average computer screen rarely offers better than 96 dpi.)

A s a general rule, it is harder to read text on-screen than on the printed page.

 Most people – irrespective of age or reading competence – find reading from a screen quite difficult. It is more difficult and more tiring than reading from a book, magazine or newspaper.

The font makes a difference, too. Sans serif fonts (such as **Arial**) are easier to read on screen, but fonts with serifs (such as the font you are reading now) work better on paper.

But there are benefits from reading text on a computer screen. The font size of text on screens can often be enlarged, or set on a differently-coloured background, which can help some pupils with reading difficulties.

If reading from the Internet, you may have the option to view a text-only version of a website. You could also resize the browser window, making it narrower. This can help in reducing the line lengths of text, lowering the chances of getting lost whilst reading.

Text can also be copied from a website and pasted into a more flexible software application, such as a word processor. I regularly use Microsoft Word in this way: pasting text into Word as unformatted text gives me more control over how I can view it – and hence read it – on-screen.

 Many people also find it easier to read text on-screen if it's white on a dark background – an option with some software (such as Microsoft Word) – because there is less glare.

If pupils are happy to read on-screen, fine. If not, get it printed out for them. Be prepared for a child to print anything they want to read (or you want them to read), if they are more comfortable reading on paper.

Non-fiction books

And so, having looked at other information sources, on to non-fiction books.

Non-fiction is, of course, anything in prose which doesn't tell a made-up story. It provides information.

Some children – especially boys – don't 'get on' with fiction, but can be converted to the reading habit by being introduced to good, entertaining non-fiction books on subjects which grab them.

Many a small boy will read anything he can lay his hands on about dinosaurs, for example. Hard-bitten young people who wouldn't dream of reading a 'soppy' story will often happily read books or other reading material about sport and sports people too.

Words and pictures

Illustrations are very important in non-fiction books.

Later, you will need to find non-fiction books for developing (and developed?) readers that include something meaty to read, as well as being well-illustrated.

But be reasonable. When you read, say, a history book – or pick it up to decide whether you want to read it – what do you look at first?

Many information books are, in fact, little more than picture books with captions. And that's fine when you are trying to harness visual literacy as a way into print reading.

Almost certainly you look first at the cover (which is invariably illustrated), the illustrations and any photographs. Children are no different.

Naturally, the youngest children, or those who have furthest to travel in their reading, need more pictures and less writing.

 Nicholas Allan's witty *Where Willy Went*, published in 2004 and which teaches the basics of sex education for under-7s (or anyone else!) is an outstanding example of getting the balance right for beginner readers.

 The skill is to manage the transition from pictures to text and to ease the reader on to an increasing amount of text, as their reading ability builds.

Choosing non-fiction titles

Even the youngest children can be encouraged to acquire an interest in non-fiction books.

 For example, take Nicola Davies's splendid 2005 book *Poo: A Natural History of the Unmentionable*. It's a fascinating exploration of the function of excrement in the animal kingdom and most children love it because it's off-beat and deals cheerfully with the 'unmentionable.' A mini-edition entitled *Poo: Mini Edition: A Natural History of the Unmentionable* came out in 2006.

Nicola Davies – an author who has campaigned widely for non-fiction to be given higher status as part of children's reading – has written many other engaging books too, such as *Oceans and Seas*.

There are also many other excellent books available, especially on art and how to do it, horses, space, animals, and music and how to make it. And Sam

For some children, non-fiction books can be more compelling than fiction.

and Susan Stern have written some sparky titles about food, nutrition, health and cookery.

The Practical Teaching Ideas section which follows (pages 162 to 186) contains many non-fiction reading suggestions for children of different ages.

Over 12s are often happy dipping into adult non-fiction books but, if they aren't, a trawl through the children's books/hobbies and interests section on *www.amazon.uk*, or one of Amazon's other sites, will suggest plenty of titles, topics and authors.

Some titles will, of course, be related to the curriculum, but don't be afraid to go outside it.

> The very best reason for a child wanting to read a non-fiction book is because it is about something which interests them.

And *any* reading helps to develop reading skills and establish the reading habit.

Tap in to what grabs them

Sometimes a child who is otherwise turned off by reading will avidly consume anything written about a favourite subject (or obsession) of theirs. So this can be an ideal starting point for a reluctant reader.

So, if you want to encourage children to read non-fiction, start by finding out what they are interested in.

 In a London comprehensive I once taught a boy who was in love with buses. I think he knew every bus route in London. If you wanted to make a bus journey, it was certainly easier to ask him how to get somewhere than to look at a timetable.

Although bright, he wasn't a keen reader. But he would, of course, read anything concerned with buses – so *that* was a way into reading for him.

(When he left school, he was offered an administrative job with what was then London Transport – where I'm sure he was a great asset!)

There are many different kinds of non-fiction topics that can grab children, and you should be able to find books on most subjects without too much difficulty.

If you talk to young people about biography and autobiography, many will tell you that they like reading about sports personalities. Some of these are biography and some are autobiography (although the 'autobiographical' ones are often actually written by a professional known as a 'ghost writer').

Some are about sporting legends of the past such as W. G. Grace and Bobby Moore. Others are about, or by, more recent sports achievers such as Wayne Rooney and Tim Henman.

Other popular topics include animals, travel and history. There are a lot of youngster-friendly books around on the Romans, Tudors and Victorians

– because these topics feature prominently in the primary curriculum in the UK – and on the twentieth century dictators (which currently dominate the history curriculum in secondary schools).

Some good non-fiction books are suggested in the practical teaching ideas section (pages 162 – 186).

7 Reading for Information

Practical Teaching Ideas

Reference books

Finding information in reference books relates as much to study skills as to developing reading. However, reading for information is also a skill in itself. Children need to learn how to read a text and identify the information that they are looking for.

✐ You may need to reinforce knowledge of the alphabet, because in many cases using reference books and indexes in books depends on it.

This may mean going back to the alphabet song or, with older pupils, using some other way.

Make sure that children know how to find simple bits of information from reference books. Show them how to do it.

Once a child gets into the habit of turning to reference books, don't prevent them from browsing or dipping.

If something interesting catches the eye, then there's immediate motivation to read it – even it if wasn't the reason for turning to the book in the first place.

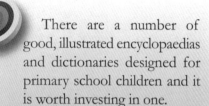

Parents at home can do much to help in this regard, by making sure that their children have ready access to a dictionary or a concise encyclopaedia.

There are a number of good, illustrated encyclopaedias and dictionaries designed for primary school children and it is worth investing in one.

Newspapers

Many pupils will come to school with little or no experience of newspapers, and they will not be used to seeing adults reading them.

So, to compensate, you need to make plenty of newspapers available in school. You will also probably need to show pupils how they are structured – with front page news, editorial, comment, features, sports pages, etc.

Getting newspapers into school

Shop around for a good deal. Some newspaper publishers are so keen to hook young readers that they will sometimes subsidise newspapers in schools.

You could ask your local newsagent for a reduced price if you buy several papers each day.

Reading newspapers is a great habit to acquire.

✏ Many accountancy practices, legal firms or similar businesses subscribe to newspapers to place in their reception, for visitors to read. Ask them to keep these newspapers for you, rather than throwing them out at the end of the day. A one-day-old newspaper is better than none.

✏ Or you could take your own newspaper to school with you and ask colleagues to do the same.

⚙ Reading newspapers

✏ Don't worry about the (often snobbish) difference between 'quality' newspapers and the rest. Just encourage the children to read at their own level.

- Actually, every paper is informative and helps to build up reading stamina – even if it also has a lot of pictures and is stronger on celebrities than hard news.

It really doesn't matter whether, in the UK for example, a child chooses to read *The Sun* or *The Guardian*. The aim is to find ways to develop reading and build reading stamina; from this point of view, *what* they read is rather less important.

- In any event, many students will start with an easy-read, accessible paper and move on to something more challenging as they get older and/or when they feel ready.

Don't push it. Just be positive about newspaper reading in general, and chat to them about things you and they have read in newspapers.

Younger readers, or those who really find large, adult newspapers off-putting, might try *First News* (*www.firstnews.co.uk*). It is a weekly UK newspaper for children, available in newsagents. It is very child-friendly and accessible.

- Newspapers are also something you might want to consider if you are a parent. A daily newspaper in the home could, with the right encouragement, help your Leo or Lily with literacy.

Magazines

Unlike newspapers, magazines appeal to a much more specialist interest. Success therefore is likely to require matching the right magazine with the right child.

Getting magazines into school

Buying large numbers of magazines is expensive. But you can often collect back-copies free.

 Find out what your colleagues regularly buy or subscribe to. They may be willing to give you magazines they have finished with.

Can parents help by donating back copies of specific magazines?

> Almost all magazines are considerably cheaper on subscription than if you pay for them as you go along – a point worth bearing in mind for both teachers and parents.

Talk to your newsagent. Unsold magazines are usually returned to the supplier, but you may be able to persuade your friendly newsagent to save a few for your school.

Reading magazines

Ensure that the children appreciate that magazines don't need to be read sequentially, starting at the beginning. It's also not necessary to read all of a magazine.

Encourage the children to browse through the magazine, identifying articles or features that might interest them.

It makes good sense to chat to pupils about which magazine titles they would like to see in school.

 If they start reading an article but don't finish it, don't worry. At least they are reading.

> Think about how you browse magazines. Don't expect more from a child.

 Reading advertisements can be a very useful way 'into' a magazine. If a child is really interested in a topic (e.g. fishing), they are likely to be attracted by adverts for fishing equipment, for example.

The Internet

 Encourage children to make the most of the Internet. Every time they use Google or some other search engine, they are actually reading. The Internet has a key role in reading development.

 Computer games are generally a different matter. Most use little or no written text – although some (e.g. the Nintendo DS) have written instructions that can motivate struggling readers (they need to read and follow the instructions to be able to get to higher levels in the game).

> From a reading development point of view, games are of limited value.

Another way of using the Internet to develop reading is to lead children to sites offering quite substantial blocks of written text and then giving them time and space to read them.

The BBC on-line

Introduce your children to the BBC News website at *news.bbc.co.uk*. An electronic whiteboard would be an ideal way to do this, if you have access to one, because then you can work with a group rather than an individual or a pair of children.

It's an excellent news site, offering both news and background, which covers a wide range of areas:

✓ World	✓ Politics
✓ UK	✓ Health
✓ Northern Ireland	✓ Education
✓ Scotland	✓ Science/Nature
✓ Wales	✓ Technology
✓ Business	✓ Entertainment.

> There are photographs, maps and diagrams to make the meaning of the news stories clear. The pages are uncluttered by advertising, and the latest headlines continually run across the top. It is a good source of reading.

One good way of encouraging pupils to read carefully from this site, and to learn their way around it, is to set some key questions and charge them with finding the answers on the website.

You could also make children aware of the main BBC website – *www.bbc.co.uk*, where they can read about their favourite television and radio programmes (as well as much more).

✍ Point them in the direction of the two BBC portals designed for children, too: *Cbeebies* (for very young children) and *CBBC* (for older children) offer games, activities, information and social networking.

Other useful sites

✍ If, for instance, a child is learning about **Ancient Egypt** at school, they would find the information at *www.ancientegypt.co.uk* interesting and worthwhile – it's part of the British Museum's education work. There's plenty there to read and the illustrations are good.

✍ Or, for example, a ten year-old wanting information about animal conservation across the world would find good reading material on the **World Wildlife Fund** website *www.wwf.org.uk*.

✍ **Wikipedia** (available in many languages, but in English at *http://en.wikipedia.org/*) offers huge amounts of reference text on a staggering range of topics.

Some of the articles on Wikipedia can be quite difficult or technical, but it is a great place to start when looking up anything, from soap stars' birthdays to scientific explanations.

✍ **The National Trust** *www.nationaltrust.org.uk*. The 'families and children' section of Learning and Discovery has excellent reading for young children, including Trusty the Hedgehog. Elsewhere on the site is good heritage information for secondary students.

✍ The Royal Society for the Protection of Cruelty to Animals (**RSPCA**) *www.rspca.org.uk* has an Animal Action Club Online linked to the RSPCA's print magazine *Animal Action* (another one for the library?) which is aimed at under 13s.

✐ **The International Save the Children Alliance** *www.savethechildren.net* is full of good reading about education across the world.

 ## Other uses for the Internet

You can also help children to use the Internet to find reading matter about famous people past and present, films, plays, music and even books – which takes us back to the basis of reading.

✐ If, for example, children have seen a film and want to know more about its cast, plot, director or how it was made, typing the name of the film into a search engine such as Google will throw up useful websites with plenty to read.

> This is especially true if it's a well-known or cult film, such as *Lord of the Rings*, *Charlotte's Web*, *The Wizard of Oz* or one of the *Shrek*, *Wallace and Gromit* or *Pirates of the Caribbean* films.

Many newly-released films also have their own dedicated websites. Wikipedia is also a good port of call for information on classic films. You can often get fascinating background information

 Most young people are more likely to read short life-stories on-line than to pick up a book-length biography.

The Internet has a lot of information about famous people from the past, on history and other websites – from Tutankhamen, Hadrian and Pythagoras to Helen Keller, Martin Luther King, Nelson Mandela, Marilyn Monroe and Douglas Bader – all of whom are likely to arise in curriculum work as well as being general interest topics.

on such movies from Wikipedia – including, sometimes, information the movie companies would prefer that you didn't know!

✎ Similarly if they want, or need, to know about music and musicians, there are plenty of websites to provide reading material.

 ## E-books

E-books, or electronic books, are a relatively new arrival on the digital scene. A number of dedicated e-book readers are now available (e.g. Amazon's Kindle and the Sony eBook Reader).

Software 'readers' are also available for a range of devices, ranging from desktop computers to mobile phones, tablet computers and even games consoles. All of these devices are able to read digital books, or e-books, which can be downloaded from the Internet.

Although most e-books, like their paper versions, must be purchased, many classic (i.e. out of copyright) novels can now be downloaded free of charge from the Internet.

 For example, novels by Charles Dickens, Shakespeare, Mark Twain and Edgar Allen Poe are all available as free e-book downloads.

 ## Where to obtain e-books

✎ Many e-books can be purchased direct from publisher's websites, or from on-line e-book retailers such as *www.e-books.com*. As the market grows, more e-book retailers will no doubt emerge.

It's probably a good idea to start with a few free e-books, to see if the format appeals.

✎ The following are just some of the sites where free e-books can be downloaded.

✓ **Project Gutenberg** (*www.gutenberg.org*) has the largest collection of public domain (i.e. out of copyright) e-books, with over 30,000 e-books held (at the time of writing).

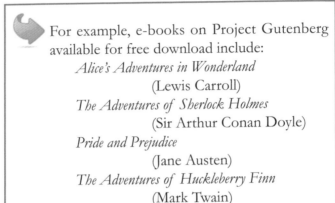

For example, e-books on Project Gutenberg available for free download include:

Alice's Adventures in Wonderland
(Lewis Carroll)

The Adventures of Sherlock Holmes
(Sir Arthur Conan Doyle)

Pride and Prejudice
(Jane Austen)

The Adventures of Huckleberry Finn
(Mark Twain)

Dracula (Bram Stoker)

The Importance of Being Earnest
(Oscar Wilde)

✓ *www.scribd.com*
✓ *www.getfreebooks.com*
✓ *www.e-book.com.au/freebooks.htm*
✓ *www.ebookdirectory.com*
✓ *www.free-e-books.net.*

Making use of e-books

E-books offer another opportunity for children to read, and therefore they should be encouraged if children show an interest in reading in this way.

✏ However the experience of reading text on the screen – especially on the smaller, lower quality screens found on mobile phones – can be tiring (see page 156, above).

✏ Whilst encouraging children to read in this way if they want to, you should point out the shortcomings as well. If children don't get on with reading on-screen, they should appreciate that this is to do with the limitations of the technology, rather than with 'reading' itself.

✒ E-books seem to me to offer a perfect opportunity for two kinds of reader in particular:

✓ Keen readers, who want to be able to read whenever the opportunity arises. Such readers might, for example, use their mobile phone to read (e.g. in the bus queue, waiting to be picked up by a parent, etc.) in situations where they might not always have a book with them.

✓ Very reluctant readers (especially boys), who are unwilling to pick up and read a book. They may be willing to read on a screen – simply because computers and technology are 'cool', even if the reading experience is in fact worse.

 # Non-fiction books

Reading non-fiction

✒ Encourage children to read non-fiction books, not just as points of reference when they want to know something specific, but as 'reading texts' to be carried around and enjoyed.

✒ Introduce non-fiction books to children as early as you can.

✒ Be seen with biographies, books on history, science, travel and anything else which interests you.

One child might read, say, a book that ties in with a TV wildlife documentary series, while next to them is another who is absorbed in a novel.

Make sure that you role-model reading non-fiction, too.

Chat to the children about your choices and your responses to the books, when you have read them.

✒ Put plenty of non-fiction books in the classroom and/or library for the child who isn't fictionally inclined, and as an alternative for everyone else. After all, reading is reading.

> As they progress through school, most children will gradually learn to cope with a balance tilting toward more text and less illustration. But to start, just a few words on each page might be what they need.

✒ Browse in bookshops and use the 'look inside' facility offered by some Internet booksellers (e.g. Amazon) to find other books that give interesting information presented in an engaging and accessible way.

✒ Whatever the age or reading ability of the young people you are working with, involve them in helping to choose non-fiction books to buy for the school. Look at print or on-line catalogues with them. Ask them about 'new' topics they would like to read about.

Get into the habit of doing a mental word count when you look at a page of text.

If you want children to develop their reading you need at least 150 – 250 words per page for reasonably competent readers under 11.

Reading non-fiction isn't just for school.
It's a great way for parents to share their children's interests and passions.

 ## Non-fiction as 'stories'

Sometimes the line between fiction and non-fiction can get pretty blurred, because in fact the best non-fiction also tells a 'story.' Here are some good non-fiction 'story' books.

✓ *1000 Inventions and Discoveries* by Roger Bridgman (Dorling Kindersley) is full of well-told stories, including how Henry Ford came up with his idea for the first mass-produced car, how James Dyson invented a new vacuum cleaner and how the television was invented.

✓ Or take *Pirates, Plants and Plunder!* in which Stewart Ross, a fine writer of non-fiction for children, tells half-invented, action-packed, fact-based stories about people in history connected with plants. It's an ingenious idea that results in a set of spiky tales which demand attention, because Ross brings out the drama and the romance.

What about Rosemary Sutcliff's splendid Roman novels (*The Eagle of the Ninth*, *The Silver Branch* and *The Lantern Bearers*) reissued by Oxford University Press in 2007? Or Elizabeth Laird's newer *Oranges in No Man's Land*?

Both are fiction, but told from a non-fiction point of view. They are splendid information sources about Roman Britain and war-torn 1980s Beirut respectively.

 ## An appealing non-fiction book

I recommend that you put a copy of the well-illustrated, annually updated *Whitaker's World Book of Facts*, edited by Russell Ash, in your classroom.

There is a fact in every sentence of this thematic (rather than alphabetic) encyclopaedia and eclectic book. For example, in the *Building and Structure* chapter, a double page spread is devoted to Bridges and Tunnels. We learn that The Golden Gate Bridge in San Francisco was the world's longest bridge for many years after it was built in 1937. Today the longest bridge is the Akashi Kaikyo Bridge in Japan. The page also tells you about very old bridges such as Ironbridge in Shropshire in the UK (1781) and the Bridge of Sighs in Venice (1560).

The *Language and Literature* chapter has a good page on the world's different alphabets, for example, as well as on Braille — and lots more beside.

Books like this score with children partly because they're quirky and interesting, but also because they are 'dip-in' books. No one expects the child to read *Whitaker's World Book of Facts* from cover to cover, so from the child's point of view it's an unpressurised read.

A lot of fine non-fiction is published every year. Don't neglect it. Make it an important part of how you develop your children's reading.

Tap in to what grabs them

 ### Finding 'hooks'

Finding the subjects that 'hook' individual children is the key to unlocking non-fiction reading.

- So try to establish chatty and less formal relationships with your students, so that you learn what they are interested in.

It's all another take on 'start where the pupil is at.'

- But if you teach large numbers of children, this isn't always easy. So encourage your colleagues – classroom, teaching and learning assistants – to do the same. Then, as a team, you stand a good chance of knowing what turns the children on.

 And it isn't always predictable. I have worked with pupils potty about equally unlikely topics such as Marilyn Monroe, sharks, English folk-dancing, bull terriers, black and white films and the life and times of Charles Dickens – as well as the ubiquitous football teams and pop bands.

And a lot of boys are just mad about giant machines.

Once you know what interests individual children, you can make sure that there are plenty of books available on 'their' topics.

 ## Promoting special interests

Try devoting a lesson or two to having the children tell each other about their special interests.

 Start by telling the group about one or two of *your* interests. Be as off-beat as you can.

> If it were me, I might talk about passions such as goats, *The Nutcracker*, lily of the valley or Monet's paintings. (A bit like *These are a Few of my Favourite Things* from *The Sound of Music*.)

I would point out that you can, of course, get books on all 'my' interests and I have indeed read lots of them. Show the children a few books relevant to your special interests.

Then get them to take turns to say what their own special interests are. This is a good speaking and listening activity. It is also an excellent way of 'researching' children's potential reading topics. Make an unobtrusive note of the subjects they pick.

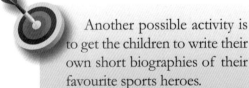

Another possible activity is to get the children to write their own short biographies of their favourite sports heroes.

They can then swap them amongst themselves and read each other's. This can be a real encouragement to them to read.

✎ Afterwards you might invite the girl who is mad about aircraft (or toads), or the boy who is fascinated by space exploration (or baseball), to help you choose some suitable books on the subject for the school library. Involve as many children as you can.

✎ Later, another speaking and listening lesson could include these children talking to the group about the non-fiction books they helped to order and have now read – to encourage others to read them too.

You can promote special interests in this way with children of any age.

Life stories

Life stories (including biographies and autobiographies) is a popular genre. Any bookshop will have a large selection. So will Amazon and other book-shop sites.

> Teenagers able to read fluently will often read or dip into books intended for adults, if they are drawn to the subject.

The children, and you, should browse regularly in the biography section of the school (and possibly the public) library. Study the biography areas of websites about books, too. Book blogs are good sources of recommendations, as well.

> It's harder to find good sport biographies for younger readers. But you can help them to read sections of the books meant for older readers and/or read sections aloud to them.

✓ Look for good series such as Hodder Wayland's *Scientists Who Made History*, which includes books on Alexander Graham Bell, Leonardo Da Vinci and Einstein.

✓ Or Heinemann Library's *Writers Uncovered*, which has books on Jacqueline Wilson and Terry Pratchett, or *Famous Lives*, which features people like Shakespeare and Ho Chi Minh.

✓ Another good example is the small, but growing, series of biographies for 7 – 11 year-olds published by Dorling Kindersley. It includes titles on Helen Keller, Nelson Mandela, Diana Princess of Wales and Gandhi – so there is plenty of multicultural interest and history here. And the books are pleasingly illustrated, but still include whole pages of text.

✓ Many quite young children have enjoyed Roald Dahl's books about his childhood: *Boy* and *Going Solo*. They also often like *War Boy: A Wartime Childhood* by Michael Foreman, because his illustrations are so familiar to children.

✓ *Barack Obama: Hope for the World* by Tim Alexander (Orion) could be useful too. It is full of information and the photographs make it pretty accessible.

✓ And pupils who have enjoyed Michael Morpurgo's many novels and stories might like *Dear Mr Morpingo: Inside the world of Michael Morpurgo* by Geoff Fox.

> For older, more accomplished readers, *Anne Frank: The Diary of a Young Girl* (definitive version) is probably one of the most remarkable autobiographical books ever written.

✓ And older (16+) students who can read fluently usually like horrifying stories of terrible childhoods, such as *Angela's Ashes* by Frank McCourt or *A Child called 'It'* by Dave Pelzer.

✓ It is also worth encouraging older students to read Bill Bryson's thoughtful and entertaining books. His autobiographical *The Life and Times of the Thunderbolt Kid* (2006) is one of his best.

Animal books

As well as all those whimsical, anthropomorphic fiction stories involving animals, try to make available some 'straight' non-fiction books about animals, too.

- ✓ Those by Gerald Durrell, James Herriot and David Taylor, for example, have stood the test of time and are funny, as well as informative.

- ✓ J. H. Williams' books about his dealings with elephants in Burma in the 1930s and 40s, especially *Elephant Bill*, still fascinate some young readers. And the late Steve Irwin wrote extensively and entertainingly about his work with crocodiles.

- ✓ Books to accompany TV wildlife series such as *Planet Earth*, or anything else by David Attenborough, are a good source of non-fiction narratives about animals. So are Jane Goodall's books about apes, such as *My Life with the Chimpanzees*, as is *Gorillas in the Mist* by Dian Fossey.

If you like reading about animals yourself, talk to the children about your choices. 'Did you know … ?' remarks work well.

> For example: 'Did you know that … a rhinoceros has a bone in its penis, a rabbit's teeth go on growing throughout its life and a duck-billed platypus has poison glands?'

Then you can tell the children where you read such strange facts and enthuse about the relevant book, website or whatever.

You can use film to stimulate interest, too. For example, the 1979 film of *Tarka the Otter*, beautifully narrated by Peter Ustinov (issued on DVD in 2006), is excellent for this purpose.

Although the story is fiction, you can talk to the children afterwards about otters, and draw from them all the 'natural history' information that is buried in the film. With help, even quite young children will be able to do this.

 Then encourage them to read Henry Williamson's book on which it is based. (They could read just sections of it if they are very young or struggling with reading.) Later, they might read *Ring of Bright Water* by Gavin Maxwell, which is also about otters.

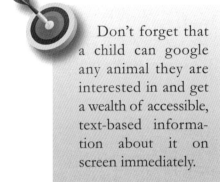 Don't forget that a child can google any animal they are interested in and get a wealth of accessible, text-based information about it on screen immediately.

 Another approach is to use 'fiction-with-information' books.

> Any child interested in reading about animals might usefully try fiction-with-information books by Brian Jacques, Dick King-Smith, Dodie Smith, Paul Gallico, Derek Tangye and many others.

Reading about the past

I f the aim is to develop reading in as many different ways as possible, history is a good starting point.

Some children, of course, will be keen to read and learn more about what they've studied in lessons – and there's nothing wrong with that.

 Make sure, though, that there are plenty of 'real' history books, as opposed to just textbooks, available.

✍ Look for attractive books about, say, the Crusades, Mutiny on The Bounty, Oliver Cromwell and the Great Fire of London. These are all good topics.

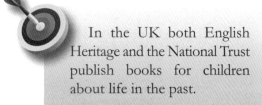

In the UK both English Heritage and the National Trust publish books for children about life in the past.

Much of what happened in history was pretty dramatic and children are quite easily engaged by it.

✍ Don't overlook historical novels either. They are billed as fiction, but of course they aren't – quite.

✓ A children's story like Mal Peet's 2006 *Penalty* (for ages 12 plus), for example, is set partly in the seventeenth century, when African slaves were being taken to South America by the Spanish. It's a history book as well as a novel.

✓ So is *King of Shadows* by Susan Cooper, which tells the story of an American boy in London who takes part in a drama project at the Globe Theatre, but gets transported through time into Tudor England. Gripping novel as it is, it's also an account of London life in Elizabethan times.

✓ Teenage students who can read well and who enjoy historical fiction will probably like adult books by Sarah Dunant, Philippa Gregory and Tracey Chevalier.

✓ Victoria Hislop's novel, *The Island*, is about leprosy in Crete in the 1930s and 40s. It's an entertaining source of information, as well as being easy to read.

✓ Other books specifically for teenagers: *The Shell House* by Linda Newbery and *Postcards from No Man's Land* by Aidan Chambers are fine evocations of the first and second world wars respectively.

✓ And, as with wildlife, TV tie-in books by authors like David Starkey, Simon Schama, Richard Holmes and Michael Wood might appeal.

 ## Travel reading

Young readers, like adults, can sometimes be persuaded to read non-fiction books, or other reading sources, about places they have visited, places they would like to visit and/or places they just want to dream about.

> When I was a child, for example, I was fascinated by the romantic and exotic sounding Tristan da Cunha. I even loved the poetry of the name. So, of course, the adults around me latched onto this and gave me articles and books to read about it – yet another aspect of developing effective literacy.

Remember, though, when you are looking for youngster-friendly travel books, that they don't actually have to be about anywhere glamorous. Experience of place starts as soon as you step across your own doorstep, after all.

✓ That's why books like James Mayhew's *Katie in London* and *The Story of London* by Richard Brassey appeal, even to developing readers living in the south of England.

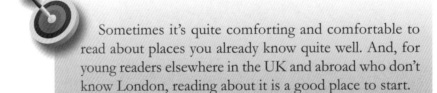 Sometimes it's quite comforting and comfortable to read about places you already know quite well. And, for young readers elsewhere in the UK and abroad who don't know London, reading about it is a good place to start.

✓ Younger readers wanting to explore more remote places in their reading might enjoy *Babar's World Tour* by Laurent de Brunhoff.

✓ For older readers, especially if they're a bit reluctant to turn to books, don't forget travel articles in newspapers, magazines and on websites.

> All newspapers give a lot of space to travel, especially in the weekend editions, and some of the articles can be quite substantial.
>
> Cutting them out and taking them to school – perhaps to put on a regularly changed notice-board – and encouraging pupils to do the same, can help promote reading.

✓ Older pupils might also like browsing in travel guides such as *Lonely Planet* or the *Rough Guides*. There is no reason why some of these books shouldn't be in the school library.

✓ And make sure the library is stocked with travel books by authors such as Chris Stewart (Spain), Peter Mayle (France), Frances Mayes (Italy) and Michael Palin (everywhere), so that there are plenty of 'place' books for older children to choose from.

The much-travelled Barnaby Bear

Barnaby Bear is a registered trademark of the UK Geographical Association (*www.geography.org.uk*). Barnaby's purpose is to teach 5 – 7 year olds about the world in a way which hooks into England's National Curriculum.

He has spawned an extensive range of books, DVDs and videos, as well as a BBC television series. There is a wide range of *Barnaby Bear* 'big books' for classroom use and ordinary 'little' books for use by individuals or for groups.

Many young children enjoy titles in the *Where in the World is Barnaby Bear?* series. It includes:

✓ *Barnaby Bear goes to Brittany*
✓ *Barnaby Bear goes to Dublin*
✓ *Barnaby Bear goes to Norway*
✓ *Barnaby Bear goes to Kenya.*

Get to know *Barnaby Bear* and introduce him to your children. He is normally presented as a way of teaching geography, but he also has the potential to develop reading. There is a designated *Barnaby Bear* website *www.barnabybear.co.uk* and he even has his own Facebook group.

8 Other Strategies for Reading

8 Other Strategies for Reading

Practical Teaching Ideas

We have looked at how children master the sophisticated skill of reading, and we have explored various ways of teaching literacy and making it stick. We have also considered, in some detail, how to work with children as individuals and how to promote reading as something exciting, worthwhile and fun.

In this chapter I want to suggest a few possible ways in which teachers can give pupils extra incentives or rewards for reading.

 ## Simple reward schemes

Some schools are experimenting with points or reward schemes (a bit like supermarket loyalty schemes) to persuade pupils to read more books and to help get them into the habit.

The idea is that the more books a child reads, the more points (or whatever it is) they get. These then lead to some sort of reward, such as prizes, certificates, 'golden time' or credit at the school bookshop.

Caught reading

✎ One school I know runs a scheme called 'Caught Reading'. If a child is 'caught reading' by a teacher or other adult at the school, they may be given a ticket with the words 'I've been caught reading' printed on it. It also has a number. The ticket is a raffle ticket, entry to a weekly school raffle (with prizes).

✎ To make this really effective, children need opportunities to pick up and read books. In the school mentioned above, racks of books are available in the school corridors, in the playground and in other shared areas.

Rewards

As a teacher, you know your pupils. What sort of reward(s) would motivate them to read more books?

You can always try to secure school funds to pay for some of the rewards, but with initiative you should be able to offer some rewards at no cost.

✎ Speak to local businesses: they may be willing to offer something once they know it is for a good cause.

✎ You could also talk to parents. Some might be working for a company that is willing to offer a little something – especially if it is in their line of business.

✎ All of the following rewards have worked for some pupils in some schools:

✓ Slices of pizza or other foods (but this may not be a good idea from a health point of view).

✓ A paid-for trip (so there is no cost to the children) to a sports event such as professional football match.

✓ A group sleep-in at school at a weekend.

✓ A paid-for theatre trip (so, again, no cost to the children).

✓ Credit at local shops (ideal if you can persuade a retail outlet to act as a sponsor).

✓ Stickers and stars (for the youngest children).

✓ Lots of public praise.

✓ Name(s) published (in school magazines, on the school Intranet, noticeboard, read out in assembly, etc.).

Accelerated Reader

The Accelerated Reader scheme, developed by the company Renaissance Learning, is one way of making it easier for schools to promote and support reading. And it's an example of rewards in action. It's an American scheme operating in 70,000 schools worldwide. In the UK, see *www.renlearn.co.uk/*.

Basically the scheme comprises software containing carefully thought-out quizzes on thousands of books – from the simplest picture book through to novels by Charles Dickens and Jane Austen.

You'll probably find that most of the books you have in your school library are included in the scheme.

First the pupil undertakes a computerised test to find out the level at which

Children seem to enjoy this approach, and in most participating schools they get rewards for reading more than a certain number of books in a particular time period, or for progressing up a level.

they should be reading. The children can then borrow and read a book at that reading level. Once the book is read, the pupil attempts a searching computer quiz which checks that the book really has been read and understood. Only then can the pupil move on to another book.

Since Accelerated Reader 'knows' the word count of every book in the scheme, it is able to keep track of the total number of words that every child has read. Each child therefore has two 'scores' – the level at which they are reading and the total number of words read. This tends to foster a competitive approach, especially amongst boys, which does promote reading.

Y ou can even reward 'word millionaires' under the scheme: children who have read a million words in total.

Sponsored reading

Some pupils will read more if they know that their reading is not only good and fun, but also making a real difference to people in need. One way of harnessing this is to hold a sponsored read. It can work for any age group.

This is what you need to do:

- Work with a single class or group, or get the support of colleagues to make it a school-wide activity.

- Identify a charity you and the pupils want to support.

- Decide whether you will allow pupils to read any book they choose, or

If you're really brave, if you have plenty of adults to help you and if can do without sleep, you could consider a 24-hour sponsored 'read-in' at a weekend!

whether to have a set list – perhaps of titles the school has multiple copies of. The choice of books could always be tied in to the charity being supported.

- Agree on a time span – say one week, two weeks or a month?

- Think of a way of certifying that each book has been read – for example, a parent or teacher could sign to confirm. Or you could set aside time in school, say every day for a month, so that you can see that the reading has been done.

- Devise the paper-work – sponsor-ship forms and checklists on which to record the reading progress.

- Encourage the pupils to have as many sponsors as possible – the simplest way is to be sponsored so much per book.

Sometimes the time spent reading can be sponsored (at, say, one penny per minute) – but this can be fiddly to monitor unless you decide that nothing less than 20 minutes counts.

However, calculating sponsorship in this way can allow slower readers to take part on an equal basis.

- Have a reasonably foolproof way of collecting the proceeds afterwards.

- Take part yourself – with sponsors – so that it becomes 'our' project.

Readathon

In the UK, another way of doing a sponsored read is to use Readathon (*www.readathon.org*), which does much of the basic work for you. It is a charity which provides support for sponsored reading and raises funds for CLIC Sargent (*www.clicsargent.org.uk*) and the Roald Dahl Foundation (*www.roalddahlfoundation.org.uk*).

Readathon, of which Roald Dahl was chairman from 1988 until his death in 1990, was started in 1984 to encourage reading. The money it raises helps children with cancer, Hodgkin's disease, leukaemia, epilepsy, blood disorders and acquired brain injury.

> Although it is ideal for Children's Book Week in October each year, you can do Readathon at any time of the year.

Readathon can supply a free pack containing:

- ✓ sponsor forms
- ✓ badges, stickers, and other extras for participants
- ✓ literacy-based project materials
- ✓ coloured posters
- ✓ an organiser's guide.

 ## Book prizes

There are several annual prizes for children's books – The Carnegie Medal, the Costa Book of the Year (formerly the Whitbread Prize), and in the US – the Newbery Medal.

> If you draw young readers' attention to these, and encourage them to read the shortlisted books before the winner is announced, it can help to promote their interest in books.

They get interested in the competition and start to care about who wins and who loses – as if it were a sports event.

This is what you need to do:

- ✐ Check relevant websites to find out exactly when a shortlist is announced.

- ✐ Make sure you know which books are on the shortlist, as soon as it is published.

- Budget funds in advance to buy copies of the books. (Can you persuade a local bookseller to sponsor this?)

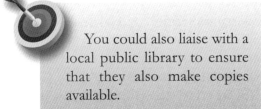

You could also liaise with a local public library to ensure that they also make copies available.

- Ideally you need about 50% more books than you have children, because they will read at different speeds and you don't want anyone left bookless.

R ead all the books yourself, too – of course.

- Know when the overall winner will be announced (check the relevant websites). That is your deadline. 'Psych' the children up to it.

- Get the children to record their responses to the books, perhaps by writing reviews, putting comments on a class/library notice-board, giving the children a proforma to complete – or whatever works for you (and them!).

- Organise a vote for the winner, the day before the announcement is due.

- On the big day, compare your votes with the 'real' winner – and discuss, celebrate, marvel, or whatever.

 ## Carnegie Medal shadowing

T he Carnegie Medal is arguably the UK's most prestigious award for a children's book.

It has been awarded each year since 1936, and past winners include *Pigeon Post* by Arthur Ransome, *The Borrowers* by Mary Norton and *The Owl Service* by Alan Garner.

The judges are all children's librarians, who announce their shortlist of five to eight books each April – chosen from books published between January and August the previous year.

The Carnegie Medal is now run by CILIP (Chartered Institute of Librarians and Information Professionals).

The winner is announced in June.

In recent years many schools have signed up to be 'official' Carnegie Medal shadowers. That means the children read the books, discuss them in their schools and post reviews on CILIP's website. CILIP provides advice and support materials for those wanting to take part.

The only resource needed is copies of the shortlisted books. Further information can be found at *www.carnegiegreenaway.org.uk/shadowingsite.*

World Book Day

World Book Day, which began in 1997, is usually on the first Thursday in March, but check from year to year as this may not always be the case.

See *www.worldbookday.com* for further information.

UK schools can register to receive packs and free book tokens worth one pound for each pupil. Each year a small number of 'bargain' books are published – usually by well-known authors. These books cost just one pound each, so there are books for pupils to spend their tokens on, if they don't want to (or can't) add any more money to the value of the token.

Sponsored in the UK and Ireland by National Book Tokens and the Booksellers' Association, World Book Day is a celebration of the importance and pleasure of books – with lots of events.

On the day, World Book Day publishes a list of quick reads to encourage and inspire 'those of us who have lost the habit of reading for pleasure, or have yet to acquire it.'

Many of your pupils will be in the latter category, so World Book Day is a very useful thing to get involved in.

 ## Library clubs

Almost all primary and secondary schools now enrich the curriculum through after-school clubs.

Make sure that in your school one of these after-schools clubs is a library club.

- The idea is to get pupils into the library (or library area, or corner) for an hour or so after school on an equal basis to read and take part in book-related activities.

- For example, they might do quizzes, design illustrations for books, write letters to authors, learn how to find what they want in the library, research book titles and authors on the Internet, listen to talks by authors or tell each other about books which have impressed them.

- In a secondary school this might be the province of the school librarian (or the teacher) who runs the library. In a smaller primary school it is likely to be any teacher with sufficient enthusiasm.

Some pupils may be very happy to turn up at the library club and simply curl up in a corner with a book they are already engaged with. That's fine. Let them do that.

Make reading a social activity whenever you can.

Others may want to talk about books and/or do something more active. The key things are to maintain their interest in books, and to keep them coming back. Ideally the pupils will have such a good time that they will tell their friends about the club, and your numbers will rise.

However you run the library club, you need a 'book nut' at the helm. Remember that the club may be competing with a football, drama or art club – all of which are potentially more attractive to young eyes.

Library club tips

- Get as many other adults as you can to come along – it shows that reading is not exclusive to librarians and English teachers.

- Invite classroom assistants and domestic staff, as well as colleagues who teach subjects like science and PE.

> Role-modelling, as we've noted before, is a very effective way of developing the behaviour you want (in this case, good reading habits).

- Have an activity or clear focus for each club meeting.

> You might organise a literary treasure hunt (hunting for different characters and locations in various books on the shelves); you might read the opening of a really gripping book aloud (such as Bernard Ashley's *The Little Soldier*, Deborah Ellis's *Breadwinner*, or Beverley Naidoo's *Web of Lies*) and stop on a cliff-hanger; you might watch a short section of a DVD version of a book together, or you might get a 'non-literary' colleague (e.g. the head of ICT) to talk about their favourite book.

- Provide some refreshments, because children love getting food. A couple of packets of biscuits with something as simple as juice in a paper cup will do.

> Find a way of budgeting for this – it's a small investment and really helps to make your club feel more 'clubby' and less like a lesson.

Always have something exciting planned for next week and tell the pupils about it, to encourage them to come again.

 Advertise the club and the next meeting's activity on posters around the school and/or in the weekly newsletter and/or via the school Intranet.

 Consider asking parents to come to the club too.

I f you can get parents on-side and show them what you are doing, they are more likely to support their children's reading at home.

 ## Start a reading group

Book groups have become quite popular with adults in the UK, the USA and elsewhere (in fact the plot of Karen Joy Fowler's 2005 novel *The Jane Austen Book Club* depends on it).

> The idea is that a group of people – friends, work colleagues or whatever – all read an agreed book and then meet up to have a structured discussion about their reading.

Typically, members take turns to suggest book titles to the group. Sometimes members will vote on which book they want to read for the next discussion session. Someone usually agrees to lead, or chair, the discussion.

A similar system can work very well in schools at all levels – and it's a good way or steering pupils into wider reading beyond the narrow limits of what they have to study for exams and assessments.

Once a book group is established, it makes sense to 'publish' some of the group's views about the books it has covered.

This can be done in school newsletters, on the Intranet and so on. Then its activities can help to promote reading – even to pupils who don't belong to the book group.

The maximum size for a workable book group is about ten people. If it's larger, some children are likely to be marginalised in discussion. Run more than one group if you've got lots of keen participants.

Ideally the pupils, especially those aged twelve and over, should be able to manage this themselves with minimum guidance and supervision, although a teacher can often revive a flagging discussion.

Pupils will (and should) come up with some good suggestions of their own for books to read. But do bear in mind – and point out to them – that a selected book needs to be 'meaty' enough to generate things to talk about.

But, in case you're stuck, here are a few suggestions of books which offer plenty of scope for discussion:

> *Simone's Diary* by Helena Pielichaty (8+)
> *The Cat Mummy* by Jacqueline Wilson (8+)
> *The Mozart Question* by Michael Morpurgo (10+)
> *A Gathering Light* by Jennifer Donnelly (11+)
> *The Bower Bird* by Ann Kelley (11+)
> *The Garbage King* by Elizabeth Laird (11+)
> *Just Henry* by Michelle Magorian (11+)
> *Blood Ties* by Sophie McKenzie (12+)
> *Junk* by Melvin Burgess (14+)
> *My Sister's Keeper* by Jodi Picoult (16+).

(The ages indicated are only an approximate guide.)

Possible talking points include:

✓ the plot: how it works and how the author has presented it;

✓ the characters: how they are depicted and whether they are convincing;

✓ the writer's style: what the style is (long or short sentences, whether it's written in the first or third person, etc.) – and whether the style suits the story;

✓ moral and other issues in the story;

✓ how it compares with other books.

I t's a good idea for the person leading or chairing the discussion to prepare a set of open questions to act as starting points.

For example – *'What do we like about the way the author tells this story? Does X make the right decision on page Y? What do we think of the ending?'* This will ensure that the discussion has some focus.

 # A secret struggling readers club

As mentioned earlier, *Boffin Boy* is a series of fiction stories written by David Orme and published by Ransom Publishing. The interest age is 8 – 14, but the reading age is around 6 – 7 years. The books are aimed at struggling readers.

One school that uses the books has started a *Boffin Boy* secret society. You only know about this club – and are only invited to join – if you're a struggling reader yourself. This is a neat way of turning potential shame into positive pride.

You could do this with almost any focus which unites your struggling readers. You could form a secret society for reluctant and/or struggling readers based around a book series, or named after a room or building where you meet, for example.

Cool ideas

And, finally, look for ways of keeping reading 'cool', bearing in mind that some children – particularly boys – are put off reading because it is quiet and solitary.

Try to focus on making reading more social.

Tap into whatever is exciting the children. It's hard to be prescriptive here because anything which is 'cool' at the time of writing will almost certainly be old-hat by the time you read this. The fashions and fancies of the young are very transitory – and you have to be bang up to date.

The National Literacy Trust has found in research that many boys are put off reading simply because it is a solitary activity – and this runs against the grain of 'hanging out with your mates'.

The way to do that is to talk to them. Ask them what's 'cool' and then try to find a literacy angle in it.

> You will probably need to think sports stars, rap stars, pop heroes, TV celebrities and the like – but find out from the horses' mouths what today's obsession is.

Having said that, trading cards, for example, seem to be a recurrent favourite – although the exact type of cards seems to change constantly.

Yet many of these cards offer 'Top Trumps'-style scores and rankings – all of which need to be read by the children. If you can't find anything else, that seems a good place to start reading.

Appendices

Resources, Suggestions and Sources of Further Information

Finally, listed here are sources of further information.

Whether you are still teaching the rudiments of decoding, or moving on to embedding fragile new skills to develop lifetime readers and achievers, I have added (at the end) a few suggestions for books which, in my experience, work well with different age groups when you are trying to build reading stamina.

 ## Phonics schemes

There are at least 20 schemes on the market and in use in schools in the UK to teach phonics. Those mentioned here are just a small selection.

More are listed at *www.standards.dcsf.gov.uk/phonics*, although they are not endorsed by the UK's Department for Children, Schools and Families. Companies are merely invited to list their products on the website if they wish.

Jolly Phonics

This is a synthetic phonics scheme which teaches the main sounds used in English and links them to the various written alphabet letters, or pairs of letters, used to represent them. There are 27 resource books and other materials for use by children learning to read and write, or to be used by parents and home educators, as well as teachers in schools.

The scheme and associated materials were designed and developed by two teachers, Sue Lloyd and Sara Wernham, from their work in a Suffolk primary school.

> Contact: Jolly Learning Ltd.
> 020 8501 0405
> *www.jollylearning.co.uk*

 ## Read Write Inc.

Ruth Miskin was a primary school teacher for 25 years, including 12 as a head teacher. As a practising teacher she developed her own method, based on synthetic phonics, of successfully teaching children to read and write fluently.

She now directs *Ruth Miskin Literacy Ltd.* and *Read Write Inc.*, which train teacher teams in schools in her methodology and in the use of her materials. Her companies also produce learning resources for children and teachers, published by Oxford University Press.

> Contact: Oxford University Press
> 01536 741171
> *www.oup.com/oxed/primary/rwi/*

 ## Oxford University Press (OUP)

As well as publishing Ruth Miskin's materials, OUP offers a range of other phonics-based resources for teachers and children under the *Oxford Reading Tree* banner. Titles and series include *Floppy's Phonics*, *Tree Tops Junior Reading* and *Oxford Magic Page*.

> Contact: Oxford University Press
> 01865 556767
> *www.oup.com/oxed/primary/oxfordreadingtree/*

 ## Sounds-Write

This is a synthetic phonics-based programme which, like *Jolly Phonics*, is based upon teaching the sounds used in spoken English. It is a structured scheme based, as Sounds-Write describes it, 'on the conceptual understanding needed to become an effective reader.' It progresses systematically to show the linking of the approximately 176 individual or compounded symbols used in writing to express sounds in English.

The scheme is currently operating in schools in six English local authorities, as well as in some schools in Northern Ireland, The Republic of Ireland and Australia. It describes itself as 'fully-integrated' with the requirements of the Literacy Hour for English schools.

> Contact: Sounds-Write
> 0845 121 7213
> *www.sounds-write.co.uk*

 ## Debbie Hepplewhite/Phonics International

Ms Hepplewhite is a former teacher and head teacher who has done much to encourage and develop awareness of synthetic phonics. She is an accredited presenter for both *Jolly Phonics* and *Read Write Inc.* (see above), as well as working as an independent consultant and trainer. She is the author of many articles in the education press about synthetic phonics and learning to read.

Her main work is an on-line, twelve-part, synthetic phonics programme for schools, parents and home educators. The first part can be downloaded from the Internet free of charge.

> Contact: Phonics International
> 01635 524911
> *www.phonicsinternational.com*

Books and other resources for teachers

Encouraging Reading by Susan Elkin (Continuum 2007)
ISBN 978-1-85539-350-9

Getting the Buggers to Read by Claire Senior (Continuum 2005)
ISBN 978-082647-347-9

Literacy: what works? by Sue Palmer & Pie Corbett (Nelson Thornes 2003)
ISBN 978-074878-519-3

Oxford Companion to Children's Literature by Humphrey Carpenter & Mari Prichard (OUP 1999)
ISBN 978-019860-228-6

 ## Reading Rockets

Reading Rockets is an American organisation based in Virginia. Its website provides a lot of free information for teachers and parents wanting to 'launch young readers', along with tips and strategies for helping 'kids who struggle'. Also on the site are many practical articles and a section devoted to finding great books and authors.

Contact: *www.readingrockets.org*

Useful organisations

 ## The UK

 ## National Literacy Trust

The National Literacy Trust is an independent UK charity dedicated to raising literacy standards for all age groups. The comprehensive and extensive website indicates how the Trust is involved directly with practical initiatives such as 'Reading Is Fundamental' (*www.rif.org.uk*) which, in the UK, gives children access to free books through local suppliers.

> Contact   National Literacy Trust
> 020 7587 1842
> *www.literacytrust.org.uk*

 ## Booktrust

Booktrust is an independent, British educational charity founded to promote the enjoyment of reading and books. It aims to encourage readers of all ages and cultures to discover and enjoy books. There is a strong focus on children's reading, and Booktrust administers a number of book prizes and awards.

> Contact   Booktrust
> 020 8516 2977
> *www.booktrust.org.uk*

 ## The Federation of Children's Book Groups

The Federation of Children's Book Groups is a UK national, voluntary organisation which promotes enjoyment and interest in children's books and reading. Local book groups organise a variety of activities in their areas, often in conjunction with, or in support of, their local schools and libraries.

Activities include authors and illustrators in schools, story-telling sessions and other book-related activities for children.

> Contact   The Federation of Children's Book Groups
> 0113 258 8910
> *www.fcbg.org.uk*

 ## UK Children's Books

This is a guide to the on-line world of children's books, providing lists of authors, illustrators and publishers, with links to their websites. A useful tool for the classroom and for children researching biographical information of their favourite authors and illustrators.

> Contact: *www.ukchildrensbooks.co.uk*

 ## Scottish Book Trust

The Scottish Book Trust organises training and outreach, children's book information, book awards and events and best of books. It runs the 'Writers in Scotland' scheme which subsidises about 2,000 author events each year. The site lists local authors registered with the scheme with a short biography, bibliography and an indication of the age range that they write for.

> Contact   Scottish Book Trust
> 0131 524 0160
> *www.scottishbooktrust.com*

 ## Australasia

The Australian Literacy Educators' Association (*www.alea.edu.au*) has useful information, although you may need to join the association to access the best of it.

See also Standards for Teachers of English Language and Literacy in Australia (STELLA) (*www.stella.org.au*) and My Read (*www.myread.org*), another Australian organisation which supports teachers of underperforming students in the middle years (ages 8 – 13).

Read Australia (*www.readaustralia.com*) is focused on teaching children to read at home. This site shows parents anywhere what they need to do to help their children read and spell. It also gives advice about where to find literacy training and workshops in Australia.

Literacy Online (*literacyonline.tki.org.nz*) is designed to support the New Zealand National Curriculum, but offers resources and ideas which would work for teachers and parents anywhere. Its aim is to help teachers develop teaching and learning programmes based on the literacy needs of their learners.

Training (UK)

Anne Harding Training

Anne Harding Training specialises in the promotion of reading at Key Stages 2 and 3, and offers a wide range of courses about the practical things you can do in your school. The company has worked in most London boroughs and for many local authorities elsewhere. Courses can be adapted – or tailor-made – to suit specific needs.

> Contact   Anne Harding Training
> 020 8959 7030
> *www.anneharding.net*

The School Library Association

The School Library Association runs a wide range of regional one-day courses aimed at school librarians and others involved in the promotion of reading in schools. There is also an annual weekend course. There are discounts on fees for SLA members.

> Contact   School Library Association
> 01793 791787
> *www.sla.org.uk*

 ## Sue Palmer

Sue Palmer, author, teacher and journalist is probably Britain's best known literacy specialist. Author of the very interesting *Toxic Childhood* (Orion 2007) and many other titles, she offers a good range of whole- and half-day reading-related courses for schools.

> Contact   www.suepalmer.co.uk
> enquiries@toxicchildhood.co.uk
> *www.suepalmer.co.uk*

Specific children's reading suggestions

 ## Key Stage 1 (ages 5 – 7)

There are many hundreds of books which very young children love sharing. You will have your own favourites and so will the children. Here are just a few possibilities.

Like many books at this level, these all, in their different ways, have wonderful illustrations:

> *Jinnie Ghost* by Jane Ray and Berlie Doherty
> *Rosie's Walk* by Pat Hutchins
> *Lost and Found* by Oliver Jeffers
> *Miffy* by Dick Bruna
> *Russell the Sheep* by Rob Scotton
> *Ten Little Rubber Ducks* by Eric Carle
> *The Big Sneeze* by Ruth Brown.
>
> Slightly older children might like:
>
> *James and the Giant Peach* by Roald Dahl
> *Just So Stories* by Rudyard Kipling
> *Mixed up Fairy Tales* by Hilary Robinson and
>   Nick Sharratt
> *The Gruffalo* by Julia Donaldson and Axel Scheffler
> *Mog the Forgetful Cat* by Judith Kerr.

 ## Key Stage 2 (ages 7 – 11)

Suggested titles to recommend to children are listed on the next page. Some of these are tried and tested old favourites which have become classics. Others are more recent.

> *I, Coriander* by Sally Gardner
> *The Amazing Story of Adolphus Tips* by Michael
>   Morpurgo
> *The Cat Mummy* by Jacqueline Wilson
> *A Bear called Paddington* by Michael Bond
> *Skellig* by David Almond
> *The Silver Sword* by Ian Serraillier
> *Goodnight Mister Tom* by Michelle Magorian
> *Simone's Letters* by Helena Pielichaty
> *Tom's Midnight Garden* by Philippa Pearce.

Other authors who write very well for this age group include:

> Anne Fine
> Lynne Reid Banks
> Sally Prue
> Geraldine McCaughrean
> Francesca Simon
> Sharon Creech
> Beverly Cleary
> Ursula K. Le Guin
> Anita Desai.

 ## Key Stage 3 (ages 11 – 14)

These titles might appeal to you and to your 11 – 14 year old students:

> *Private Peaceful* by Michael Morpurgo
> *Noughts and Crosses* by Malorie Blackman
> *Al Capone Does My Shirts* by Gennifer Choldenko
> *Tamar* by Mal Peet
> *Wolf* by Gillian Cross
> *The Foreshadowing* by Marcus Sedgwick
> *His Dark Materials* by Philip Pullman
>   (three books)
> *The Hobbit* by J. R. R. Tolkien.

Look too for suitable books by:

> Bernard Ashley
> Robert Westall
> Cynthia Voigt
> Robert Cormier
> Kevin Crossley-Holland
> Adele Geras
> Mildred D. Taylor
> Jill Paton Walsh
> James Riordan
> Philip Reeve.

 ## Key Stage 4 (ages 14 – 16)

Many students at this level will be studying fiction works for exams. Build on this by enthusing about other related books.

For example:

✓ *Of Mice and Men* could lead to John Steinbeck's *The Pearl*, *The Red Pony* and *East of Eden*.

✓ *Roll of Thunder, Hear My Cry* could lead to interest in the sequels and prequels in Mildred D. Taylor's series.

✓ *Cat's Eye* can inspire students to move on to other fiction by Margaret Atwood and then to other Canadian writers such as Carol Shields.

Students aged 15 upward will enjoy some of the books by these fiction writers, who specialise in the upper end of the 'children's' market:

> Aidan Chambers
> Linda Newbery
> Mal Peet
> Michelle Magorian.

They will also enjoy old favourites and classics originally written for adults, such as:

> *Gone with the Wind* by Margaret Mitchell
> *Rebecca* by Daphne du Maurier
> *Jane Eyre* by Charlotte Brontë
> *Silas Marner* by George Eliot
> *I Know Why the Caged Bird Sings*
>   by Maya Angelou.

Contemporary writers whose books (meant for adults) appeal to mid-teens include:

> Joanna Trollope
> Frederick Forsyth
> Ruth Rendell
> Stephen King
> John Grisham
> Rohinton Mistry.

Many boys in this age group still enjoy anything by Arthur Conan Doyle.

 ## Special Needs

Ransom Publishing has special expertise in books for reluctant and struggling readers who need engaging content at a low reading level. Most of Ransom's books for children are designed to appeal to specific interest ages and reading ages. Books are usually published in series, giving opportunities for further reading if the books are well-received.

For example:

✓ *Goal!* is a synthetic phonics-based reading programme based entirely around football and designed especially for older, struggling readers.

✓ *Dark Man* is an award-winning series for older readers (12 to young adult) with a reading age of 5 - 7.

> Contact   Ransom Publishing
> 01962 862 307
> *www.ransom.co.uk*

Nelson Thornes' *Fast Lane* series (*www.nelsonthornes.com/fastlane*) is aimed at children, especially boys, whose reading age is below their interest age. Each book comes with a CD (see page 83).

 # Glossary

Alliteration

Repeating the initial consonant of each word in a phrase, as in *Peter Piper picked a peck of pickled peppers ...* .

Analytic Phonics

A phonics-based way of teaching letters and sounds. It starts with whole words and focuses on their component parts. Usually starts with the beginnings of words, such as *cat, cup, car.* Then moves on to similar endings – *cup, hop, rap.*

So a child who correctly identifies *hop* and *top* by breaking them down into sounds will probably read successfully *fop* and *sop* – even where the meaning of these words isn't known.

This system works well in many cases, but is unreliable in others. For example, *bow* can be read in two ways – similar to *low* or *cow.*

Assonance

Internal rhyming within phrases or sentences, as in 'The crew flew to you.' Assonance is a type of alliteration.

Blending

Putting discrete phonemes together to make words – as in /c/, /a/ and /t/ blending to make the word *cat*.

A consonant blend occurs when two consonants are sounded one after the other – for example the /t/ and /r/ phonemes making the /tr/ sound in *trap*. They are usually found at the beginnings or endings of words (*bridge, clean, fist*).

Consonant

A sound in speech in which air from the mouth is stopped or partially stopped. All letters in English are consonants, except the five vowels a, e, i, o and u, and sometimes y.

CVC, CCVC, CCVCC

CVCs are simple Consonant-Vowel-Consonant words (*cat, pit, man*, etc.) that children first encounter when they begin reading using a synthetic phonics programme.

As children progress in synthetic phonics, they meet CCVC words (e.g. *trip, stop*) and CCVCC words (such as *stand, claps*).

Decode, decoding

Children decode a word when they use their phonics knowledge acquired so far to sound out a word (e.g. /m/, /a/, /t/ – *mat*). Some words in English are fully decodable – others are only partially decodable and their pronunciation needs to be learned.

Digraph

A digraph is a single discrete sound in English (i.e. a phoneme) that is represented by two or more letters (or graphemes). So the /oa/ sound in *boat*, for example, is a digraph.

Grapheme

A written representation of a spoken sound (or phoneme). A grapheme may consist of a single letter (e.g. 't' in *pit*) or it may be a combination of letters (e.g. 'th' in *thin*).

Literacy

There are various definitions of literacy, but they all relate to the ability to read and write.

Onset

The opening or beginning of a word, such as 'a' in *apple*, 'sh' in *shoe* or 'str' in *string*.

Phoneme

A distinct unit of sound, in any spoken language, which conveys a discrete meaning. For example the /*m*/ in *mat*, as distinguished from the /*s*/ in *sat*.

Phonics

A method of teaching reading that makes use of the fact that English is alphabetic.

Reading Age

The result obtained from a reading test. In theory an average child aged nine should show a reading age of nine. There are several different reading tests widely used by schools to achieve the reading age. There are signs that the concept of the reading age is falling out of favour.

Reluctant Reader

A person who can read but doesn't enjoy doing it. Also used to describe a person who finds reading difficult and therefore avoids doing it as much as possible.

Rhyme

The repetition of the end sound of words. The device is commonly used in poetry, for example … *fish*, … *wish*. The sounds may be the same, even though they are spelled differently, for example … *mare*, … *hair*.

Rhyme (or 'rime' - see below) is an important strand in teaching literacy because, like onset, it is one way in which children learn to hear (and see) links between words.

Rime

The American spelling of 'rhyme' and usually used in the context of 'onset and rime'.

Sight Vocabulary

The number of words that can be read by an individual 'at first sight', without word analysis. The words are recognised and understood instantly, quickly and easily.

Special Educational Needs (SEN)

A term with a very specific meaning in the United Kingdom and used more generally throughout the English-speaking world.

Its 'official' definition in the UK is '…where medical or cognitive disorders create barriers to learning and which require support for the learner on a long-term or ongoing basis.'

However it is often applied more generally to any child who experiences particular difficulty with any aspect of school work.

Struggling Reader

A person whose reading age is significantly below his or her chronological age. Struggling readers are often reluctant readers.

Synthetic Phonics

Using known, individual letter sounds put together (i.e. synthesised) in order to pronounce the whole word. For example, the individual sounds (or phonemes) /d/, /e/, /s/ and /k/ make the word *desk*. This method of synthesising words from component phonemes works with about 50% of the words in English.

Vowel

A sound in speech, more open than a consonant, in which air from the mouth is not stopped. The five vowels in English are a, e, i, o and u.

Vowel Blend

Two adjacent vowel letters that represent a single speech-sound, or phoneme. For example those in the words *meat, loud, soap*. These are specific examples of digraphs.

Index